The Thirty
Years' War

PROBLEMS IN
EUROPEAN CIVILIZATION

Under the editorial direction of
John Ratté
Amherst College

The Thirty Years' War

Second Edition

Edited and with an Introduction by

Theodore K. Rabb
Princeton University

D. C. HEATH AND COMPANY
Lexington, Massachusetts   Toronto   London

CONTENTS

v

II INTERPRETATIONS OF LEADING PARTICIPANTS

Gustavus Adolphus

Albrecht von Wallenstein

Cardinal Richelieu

Contents

INTRODUCTION

When, in May 1618, a group of Bohemian leaders launched a rebellion against the authority of the Hapsburgs, they precipitated a crisis which was to destroy the last vestiges of the medieval Holy Roman Empire. For the revolt was followed by a bitter war of reprisal which spread rapidly to involve all of Germany, and then at various times Scandinavia, the Netherlands, France, Spain, Hungary, Poland, Italy, Russia, and England. Peace within the Empire was achieved only after thirty years of fighting, and some of the combatants remained at war until 1660. In the course of the warfare the Emperor's power over the myriad independent princelings and cities of Germany was destroyed once and for all. He had been unable to exert this power effectively for centuries, and during the previous decades he had only just managed to weather crisis after crisis as the growth of Protestantism and the revival of Catholicism multiplied the differences and tensions in the Empire. Now, however, he was forced to face the onslaught of almost all of western and northern Europe, and it proved impossible to reassert or even retain his authority.

Such, in its simplest outlines, has long been considered the most obvious significance of the series of wars that raged throughout much of Europe during the early seventeenth century. It has become traditional to see the fighting from the outbreak of the Bohemian revolt to the Peace of Westphalia, from 1618 to 1648, as an entity called the Thirty Years' War, during which this transformation in the Empire took place. In recent years, however, serious doubts have been cast on the adequacy of such a German-centered view of the international conflicts of the period. It has been noted, for instance, that the Dutch speak of an eighty-year war of independence, lasting from 1568 to

1648; that for the French the important time span is the twenty-four-year war with Spain from 1635 to 1659; and that in fact there are almost as many chronological schemes as countries in Europe. Other long-held assumptions about the wars have been called into question in recent years, and for an understanding of the extent of revisionist opinions it might be well to indicate briefly the main elements of the traditional approach.

Above all, the wars of the early seventeenth century have been regarded, ever since their own day, as one of the worst catastrophes in history. The Germans in particular have come to see the period as a great national tragedy—with some justification, since nearly all the fighting took place in what is now Germany. It has also been customary to call the Thirty Years' War the last of the religious wars and to stress that its basic cause was the conflict sparked by the Reformation and Counter Reformation. Although it is admitted that other interests were at stake, and that as the war progressed idealism was overcome by political, dynastic, and other motives, nonetheless the fundamental issue is held to have been religion. Great emphasis is laid on the resurgence of Catholicism in the late sixteenth century and its clash with undaunted Protestantism. The formation of a Union of Protestant princes in the Empire in 1608, followed by the establishment of a League of Catholic princes in 1609, is seen as the crystallization of the two sides which were to fight as soon as the pretext of the Bohemian revolt presented itself. Only later, when foreigners entered the fray to plunder helpless Germany, did material aims triumph over spiritual. In the end, the war's main effects were to be the decimation of Germany and the final destruction of the Hapsburg Emperor's power in the Empire.

This interpretation obviously depends on seeing events through German eyes, and it achieved full expression during the era of rising nationalism in the mid-nineteenth century. In particular, the work of a best-selling novelist, Gustav Freytag, who wrote a popular history of Germany which portrayed the Thirty Years' War in the most lurid colors, reached a very wide public. In reaction to Freytag's emotional account, historians began to wonder whether this simple picture was sufficient. Some of them continued to uphold, in many essentials, the traditional interpretation, but others have challenged almost all of its assumptions. Even the most cherished, the assertion that the war was a moral, economic, and social catastrophe, has been denied.

In the selections in this volume, some leading exponents of the older view and their principal critics are represented. To indicate the typical approach of the traditional school, there are extracts from Freytag's popular history and from the work of a distinguished Czech historian, Anton Gindely. Gindely's history of the war, published in 1882, is perhaps the most thoroughly researched and scholarly account to argue that religion was the principal issue at stake, with political concerns only a close second.

But the reevaluation was already beginning during the last decades of the nineteenth century. One of the first assumptions to be questioned was the belief that the war had been a disaster for Germany. A later selection in this volume will describe some of the early suggestions that the economic effects were not as shattering as commonly supposed. The first major, complete reinterpretation, however, appeared in 1894, when Franz Mehring, a leading German socialist, incorporated into a long essay on Gustavus Adolphus a Marxist view of the period. Although he adopted parts of the traditional approach and considered the war primarily as a German affair and a disaster (and hence, as an ardent nationalist, he denounced Gustavus' invasion as a destructive foreign intervention), he introduced a new explanation of motives. Pointing to economic forces as the prime movers, he reshaped the usual emphasis on religious causation.

These signs of impending major revisions were by no means alone. Other German historians of the late nineteenth century were de-emphasizing religious motivation in favor of more purely political explanations. A good example of this type of approach will be found in Gustav Droysen's biography of Gustavus Adolphus. Yet for over forty years after the appearance of Mehring's essay the only aspect of the war to achieve much attention along new lines was the problem of its economic effects on Germany. As a later selection will indicate, there was a prolific scholarly dispute on this subject from the 1880s onwards. But there was little change in general accounts of the war.

Eventually, in the 1930s, two full histories of the war by C. V. Wedgwood and Georges Pagès reflected the changes in historical writing during the intervening decades. Miss Wedgwood followed closely in Gindely's footsteps in her periodization and narrative of the fighting, but in her account religious causation no longer played so prominent a part. Her conclusions, moreover, were marked by the pessimism of a generation which, disillusioned by the results of World War I, became convinced that warfare was always ultimately pointless. The book is notable primarily for the skill and grace of its narrative, and most of the time the underlying attitude is scarcely noticeable. The superb descriptive analysis with which Miss Wedgwood sets the scene in 1618 is among the best pieces of writing of its kind, and an excellent introduction to the subject of the war.

Georges Pagès, on the other hand, sought to place the conflict in its long-range setting, as a turning point between medieval and modern times. An authority on international relations in the seventeenth century, he saw the war as a key stage in the transfer of preponderance in Europe from the Hapsburgs to the French and in the emergence of new, independent states. Although he still accepted the customary periodization, explanations of motive, and concentration on events in the Empire, his book did represent the first important shift away from the narrow German viewpoint toward a broader interpretation of the significance of the war.

After World War II the complete revision of the older view began in earnest. In an article that openly proclaimed its intention to sweep aside all clichés, S. H. Steinberg challenged his predecessors on questions ranging from the duration of the "thirty years" war to the motives of the participants and the effects of the fighting. He combined a number of separate reevaluations, some going back to the 1880s, to launch an attack on the entire structure of traditional interpretations. Although, as will be seen in the selection from Carl J. Friedrich's book on the period, some historians found the revisions unacceptable, the attack has continued in recent years. In particular, an article by J. V. Polišenský, written from the standpoint of a modern Marxist, has exposed the inadequacy of the usual emphasis on Germany and has suggested a different emphasis for explanations of motive. Polišenský has broadened these suggestions in a book, *The Thirty Years' War,* which appeared early in 1972, too late for inclusion in the present work.

In conclusion, the last two items in Part I will indicate how widely interpretations of the war have varied. Selections have been included from an article by the editor of this volume which surveyed the history of the controversy over the economic effects of the war on Germany. As has been mentioned, this was the first area in which historians began to reassess the war, and since the 1880s it has been the subject of a great deal of research. Although it is only one component of a much larger problem, this particular discussion provides an excellent case study in the fluctuations of opinion about the war.

Finally, in the work of Josef Pekař, a fervently patriotic Czech historian, the reader will see the point of Polišenský's demand that the insular German view be abandoned. Here is a writer who regards the war as a decisive, tragic turning point in Czech history, and who discusses its significance with little reference to Germany. Its place in French, Dutch, Spanish, or Swedish history is fairly self-evident, and for this reason a Czech view has been chosen to indicate the diversity of interpretations that have been proposed.

As the reader will soon realize, there are hardly any selections in this volume which deal with the events of the war itself. This omission is intentional, because problems of interpretation, with one notable exception, do not loom so large in narrative passages. (The main outline of events has been provided in the Chronology, pp. xix–xxiii.) The one notable exception is the evaluation of the motives and aims of the participants. A great deal of one's view of the conflict, one's judgment of why it developed as it did, depends on one's assessment of the leading actors in the drama. Since the historian's opinion of these leaders is usually closely related to his more general conclusions, it is frequently most revealing to see how they are portrayed (a vivid example is provided by the last sentence of the selection from Wedgwood). It is highly suggestive, for instance, to note that three recent studies of prominent combatants in the war (Michael Roberts' work on Gustavus Adolphus, V. L. Tapié's on Richelieu, and Dieter Albrecht's on Maximilian of Bavaria—selections from the first two appear in the present volume, and the third is listed in the *Suggestions for Additional Reading*) all have a significant feature in common. Although they deal with three very different men, these books all conclude that, to understand their subject, one must realize that he acted largely under the pressure of events, often without any grand designs in mind. Such interpretations of the participants are by no means

common as yet, but it is not difficult to see that, if more widely applied, they would represent a revision of traditional views as radical
as the more self-consciously "new" approaches of Steinberg or
Polišenský.

The editor of this volume therefore decided it would be more useful to include selections dealing with some of the main protagonists,
rather than long passages of repetitious narrative, whose few points
of interpretation usually depend on nothing more than a rapid appraisal of the statesmen and generals involved. Consequently, the
second half of this volume (Part II) is devoted to selections which
reveal the divergence of opinion among biographers of three leading
combatants in the war: Gustavus Adolphus, King of Sweden; Albrecht
von Wallenstein, commander of the Imperial army; and Cardinal
Richelieu, chief minister of Louis XIII of France.

The traditional picture of Gustavus Adolphus as the heroic savior
of Protestantism rests on little that he himself wrote, but such problems have hardly deterred admirers like C. R. L. Fletcher. Undoubtedly the greatest national hero of Sweden, Gustavus has faced a
mixed reception from German historians. Although many have seen
him as a German hero, too, who saved both Protestantism and Germany from Hapsburg domination, others (see the introduction to the
selection from Mehring) have felt that he represented the intervention by foreigners which caused the wars to degenerate into a quest
for power. A suggestion of this last approach can be found in the
selection from Gustav Droysen who, to the indignation of Swedish historians, insisted on portraying Gustavus as a hardheaded politician,
concerned solely with Sweden's own interests. Nils Ahnlund's re-
affirmation of Gustavus' idealism, however, is much more sophisticated than his predecessors' hero-worship. The most recent account,
Michael Roberts' majestic two-volume work, while remaining highly
favorable, is an excellent example of recent trends in scholarship,
with its stress on the immediate needs and practical considerations
which were fundamental to every decision on policy.

With Wallenstein we come face to face with some of the most
baffling problems of seventeenth-century history, and possibly the
most controversial figure in German history before Bismarck. More
has been written about Wallenstein than about any other man in the

first half of the seventeenth century, and there is no room to do justice to the countless interpretations of his career that have been suggested since his own lifetime. He has been the first true German nationalist, one of the greatest of Czech nationalists, the last self-seeking mercenary captain, the redoubtable seeker of peace, the ineffectual traitor, and many others. Suffice it to say that the problems of his spectacular life, his overnight wealth and power, his grandiloquent dreams, his tentative treason and shattering collapse, have fascinated every generation and been solved by none. If any view can be called traditional, it is the one popularized by the German poet and playwright, Friedrich von Schiller, whose *Wallenstein* trilogy presented the general as a tragic, idealistic hero. During the last century modern scholarship has entered the controversies, and straightforward, one-sided portrayals such as Schiller's have been abandoned. Even Leopold von Ranke was attracted by this complex figure, and his detached assessment of the general as a man of his times remains, despite the subsequent discovery of new evidence, one of the most satisfactory accounts ever written. The selections from Josef Pekař and Heinrich Ritter von Srbik present, respectively, the most thoroughly researched criticism and the most thoroughly researched defense of Wallenstein's conduct. Pekař's massive, two-volume study of the last four years of the general's life concluded that he had been a shameless, self-centered traitor. Pekař typically added that his career was a tragedy primarily for Bohemia, not Germany. Srbik took the opposite approach in an exhaustively documented appraisal written specifically to refute Pekař. Although he acknowledged the failings of his hero, Srbik emphasized Wallenstein's idealism, his striving for peace, and his concern for the entire Empire, not just Bohemia. The reader might be interested to know that there is also a brief but brilliant evocation of the general's last months on pages 336–351 of the paperback edition of Miss Wedgwood's *The Thirty Years War.* It can be recommended strongly both as a fine piece of writing and as a lucid introduction to the personalities and problems of this dramatic episode in the war.

The differences in assessments of Richelieu have been more subtle, though he, too, has inspired both hatred and reverence. Most historians start with his *Testament Politique* as the chief source for his ideas. Though its authenticity has been much debated, it remains the closest we can come to a statement of intentions by the Cardinal himself, and one of the main problems has been how to interpret the *Testament*. The particular fascination of Richelieu for anyone interested in the war as a whole is his aptitude for serving as an unusually accurate weathervane for a historian's view of the entire conflict. Of the major combatants—the Emperor Ferdinand, Maximilian of Bavaria, John George of Saxony, Christian IV of Denmark, Gustavus Adolphus, Oxenstierna of Sweden, Wallenstein, Olivares of Spain, the Dutch Stadholder Frederick Henry, and himself—the Cardinal is the most difficult to characterize purely in terms of religious aims or idealism. All the others can be, and have been, given an idealistic label of one kind or another. Even the most cynical interpretations grudgingly find some lofty motive somewhere, usually of religion, peace, or unity. But with Richelieu, because his intervention was so obviously political, it has been easy to omit all hints of nobler aims. By his treatment of the Cardinal, therefore, the historian often reveals most clearly whether he thinks of the war as a natural struggle between France and the Hapsburgs, as a German conflict of which foreigners took advantage, as a struggle of ideals warped by the machinations of politicians, as an unavoidable explosion, a futile aberration, an irresistibly escalating local revolution, or maybe as all or none of these things.

Some of the different ways Richelieu has been interpreted are indicated by the selections from Aldous Huxley, Louis Batiffol, and V. L. Tapié. Huxley's is the hostile portrayal, often favored by literary men, of an avaricious and cunning Cardinal. Recent historians such as Batiffol and Tapié, on the other hand, convey a more compassionate characterization of an able statesman beset by fearsome problems.

The last eighty years, therefore, have witnessed considerable revisions of long-held assumptions about a crucial, formative period in early modern history. There is now little doubt that the war must be seen as a continent-wide phenomenon, influencing profoundly the history of international relations and of most European countries. Yet the revisionists have raised many more problems than they have solved. And in recent years the difficulties have only been intensified by a number of scholars who have tried to reinterpret the entirety of seventeenth-century history.

There is no space to enter into the various theories that have been propounded, but it should be noted that all perceive a great turning-point somewhere in the middle third of the century. Pointing either to the economic and demographic slowdown that overtook Europe from the 1620s on, or to the remarkable coincidence of revolts and rebellions that broke out in more than a dozen different areas between 1640 and 1660, they have suggested that there was a general "crisis" in western civilization in this period. (See T. H. Aston, ed., *Crisis in Europe 1560–1660* [New York, 1965].) The only link commonly made with the Thirty Years' War is the suggestion that the disruptions and devastations caused by the fighting helped bring about the interruption in economic and demographic growth. Yet it can be suggested that the war was very much a part of the "crisis."

If one way of viewing a crisis is to say that it marks the divide between a period of terrible unrest or upheaval and a time of settlement or relaxation, then Westphalia certainly marked the end of a crisis. Not only did it close the most anarchic and bloody period of international warfare Europe had ever seen, but it laid down a structure which many felt would prevent such breakdowns in the future. This was the first great peace congress in European history. Previously two or three warring parties would get together and settle their own problems. But at Westphalia an attempt was made to settle all outstanding disputes, everywhere, at one time. And, whatever the reality, the people of the seventeenth century *believed* that that was what had been accomplished. It was now assumed that a new, permanent, settled situation had been established, and for more than a century all further treaties, however extensive, were regarded merely as a rounding out of what had been laid down at Westphalia.

If these considerations add a new dimension to an understanding of the war, they certainly do not lessen the problems of interpretation. For even without this dimension, as the selections which follow will indicate, opinion is still deeply divided over questions of great importance, not only for an understanding of the period itself, but also for much subsequent history. On the answers to some of these questions depend far-reaching interpretations of German history, of the decline of religious zeal, the rise of power politics, the appearance of nationalism, and much else besides. Far more than a simple evaluation of a few battles is involved as one attempts to decide why these people went to war, what effects the fighting had, and even what exactly was meant by the Thirty Years' War.

[_Note:_ Some of the selections in Part I are divided into two sections, marked I and II. This indicates that they have been taken from the beginning and end of a work, section I dealing with causes and section II with effects. Although united by the basic question of the nature of the Thirty Years' War, these are separate problems, and it is important to realize that a single selection may consist of passages from opposite ends of a book, concerned with somewhat different issues.

It must also be stressed that, because the emphasis in this volume is on interpretation and not narrative, the following selections give an introduction to the _problems_ of the war, but not to the war itself. The Chronology is a brief guide, but the reader should have read at least a general survey of the period, such as that in V.H.H. Green's _Renaissance and Reformation,_ in H. Rowen's _A History of Early Modern Europe,_ in D. Ogg's _Europe in the Seventeenth Century,_ or in the _New Cambridge Modern History,_ Vol. 4. It would also be wise to read, in conjunction with this booklet, one of the histories of the Thirty Years' War, the most satisfactory in English being Georges Pagès' _The Thirty Years' War (1618–1648),_ David Maland and John Hooper, eds. (New York, 1970).

Finally, the reader should be aware that almost all footnotes have been omitted from the selections that follow.]

Chronology

1555   Peace of Augsburg, establishing that every state within Germany would follow the religion of its prince (*cuius regio eius religio*), but excluding Calvinism and forbidding the secularizaton of any further Church lands.

1556   Abdication of Charles V. Ferdinand I Emperor (until 1564, then Maximilian II until 1576).

1562–1572   Series of incidents culminate in outbreak of revolt in the Netherlands against Spanish rule.

1576–1612   Rudolf I Emperor. Numerous incidents between Protestants and Catholics in the Empire (e.g. Cologne, 1583–1585).

1589   Henry IV King of France. Spain at war with France.

1597   Maximilian I Duke of Bavaria. Ferdinand of Hapsburg Archduke of Styria.

1598   Edict of Nantes, granting toleration to the Protestant minority, ends civil strife in France. Peace of Vervins ends war between France and Spain.

1606–1607   Donauwörth incident: city taken over by Maximilian of Bavaria.

1608   Union of Protestant princes in the Empire formed under leadership of Calvinist Frederick IV, Elector Palatine.

1609   League of Catholic princes in the Empire formed under leadership of Maximilian of Bavaria.
Rudolf II grants Letter of Majesty to Bohemia, permitting free exercise of religion, so as to maintain support in face of his brother Matthias, who has already gained control of Hungary, Moravia, and Austria, part of the Hapsburgs' personal territories.
Beginning of succession crisis in Jülich-Cleves, with a Protestant and a Catholic as the eventual claimants.
Twelve-year truce between Dutch and Spaniards begins.

1610   Alliance of German Protestant princes, mainly in the West, with Henry IV of France. Henry prepares to invade; assassinated. Regency rule in France, with child Louis XIII King.

1611   Gustavus Adolphus King of Sweden, Axel Oxenstierna his chief minister. War between Denmark and Sweden (until 1613).

1612   Matthias Emperor. Obtains for his cousin Ferdinand of Styria the succession in Bohemia (1617) and Hungary (1618).

1614   Treaty of Xanten ends Jülich-Cleves dispute by compromise.

1617   Treaty of Stolbova ends war between Sweden and Russia (since 1604) heavily in Sweden's favor: the territorial settlement cuts Russia off from the Baltic.

1618   Revolt in Bohemia in face of increasing Catholic pressure from Ferdinand. Protestant Union sends troops (supplied primarily by the Duke of Savoy) under Count Ernst Mansfeld to Bohemia. He defeats Imperial forces.

1619   Ferdinand deposed from the throne of Bohemia. The head of the Protestant Union, Calvinist Frederick V, Elector Palatine (son-in-law of James I of England), elected in his place.

Matthias dies. Ferdinand of Styria becomes Emperor. Bavaria and Spain ally with Ferdinand. Spanish general Spinola invades the Palatinate (which is in a crucial position on the route of Spanish troops to the Netherlands).

1620   Treaty of Ulm takes Protestant Union out of the war.

John George, Elector of Saxony, joins Ferdinand.

Tilly, Maximilian's general, at the head of a combined Catholic League and Imperial army, defeats Frederick V's troops at the battle of the White Mountain, near Prague. Ferdinand regains control of Bohemia and the revolt is at an end.

Protestant Union dissolves.

1621   End of truce between Dutch and Spaniards.

Tilly and Spinola begin conquest of Palatinate from Frederick V.

The Margrave of Baden-Durlach and Christian of Halberstadt (Brunswick), two Protestant princes, raise armies to help Frederick V.

England sends two regiments to help Frederick.

Philip IV King of Spain: Count-Duke of Olivares chief minister.

Sweden and Poland at war.

1622   After battles of Wiesloch (Tilly defeated by Frederick's general, Mansfeld), Wimpfen (Tilly defeats Margrave of Baden-Durlach), and Höchst (Tilly defeats Christian of Halberstadt), Palatinate conquered. Mansfeld and Christian retreat to the Dutch Netherlands.

Spaniards occupy the Valtelline (key Alpine pass on the route of Spanish troops to the Netherlands). War between France and Spain.

First negotiations for an alliance between France and Bavaria.

1623   Maximilian of Bavaria takes over the Electorate of the Palatinate.

Battle of Stadtlohn: crushing defeat of Christian of Halberstadt by Tilly. League of Lyons between France, Savoy and Venice, formed to oppose Spain in the Valtelline.

1624   Richelieu comes to power in France.

Albrecht von Wallenstein, Bohemian nobleman who made a fortune in speculation after the subjugation of Bohemia, offers to raise independent Imperial army for Ferdinand, who hitherto had to rely almost entirely on Bavaria for troops. Wallenstein made Duke of Friedland and commander of the Imperial army, which is to be supported by forced contributions.

Alliance between the French, Dutch, and English; also between England, Sweden and Denmark.

1625   Christian IV, King of Denmark (and also Duke of Holstein, which makes him a prince of the Empire), enters the war with English subsidies.

Spinola captures Breda in the Netherlands.

Frederick Henry becomes Dutch Stadholder.

England and Spain at war.

1626   Wallenstein defeats Mansfeld at the Dessau Bridge, and Mansfeld flees to Hungary to join Bethlen Gabor, who is leading a revolt against Ferdinand, but who makes peace with the Emperor later the same year. Death of Christian of Halberstadt.
Tilly defeats Christian IV of Denmark at the battle of Lutter.
Treaty of Monzon between France and Spain, at which France gives up the attempt to capture the Valtelline for the time being.
England and France at war.

1627   Tilly and Wallenstein proceed with subjugation of primarily Protestant northern Germany. Mecklenburg and Pomerania conquered.
Death of Mansfeld.
France and Spain in alliance against England.

1628   Wallenstein appointed General of the Oceanic and Baltic seas, and begins attempt to make Ferdinand master of the Baltic. Besieges island city of Stralsund, key port which receives help from Denmark and Sweden. Wallenstein forced to withdraw.
War between Hapsburgs and France over succession to Dukedom of Mantua in Italy. Pope Urban VIII backs France.

1629   Treaty of Lübeck takes Denmark out of the war. Wallenstein becomes Duke of Mecklenburg.
Edict of Restitution issued by Ferdinand, ordering restoration of all Church lands taken over by Protestants since 1552 (including two archbishoprics, twelve bishoprics, and over fifty abbeys) Enforcement by Wallenstein begins. Gustavus Adolphus makes peace with Poland. England makes peace with France (but captures Quebec, not returned till 1632).

1630   Electoral Diet (meeting of the seven Electors of the Empire, who elect each Emperor, with Ferdinand) at Regensburg (Ratisbon). Electors refuse to elect Ferdinand's son King of the Romans, last step in succession to the Empire. Fearful of Wallenstein's growing power, they force Ferdinand to dismiss him. Leading agitation against Wallenstein is Maximilian of Bavaria. Father Joseph, Richelieu's emissary, active at Regensburg, and negotiations intensify for an alliance between France and Bavaria.
Gustavus Adolphus lands in Germany.
France occupies Savoy.
England makes peace with Spain.

1631   Treaty of Bärwalde between France and Sweden: Gustavus receives French subsidy and promises not to molest Catholic religion.
Treaty of Fontainebleau creates French-Bavarian military alliance.
John George of Saxony begins to form a Protestant army under the leadership of Hans von Arnim.
The Elector of Brandenburg (Gustavus' brother-in-law) joins Gustavus.
Tilly sacks Magdeburg, city allied with Gustavus.
Saxony allies with Sweden. Combined Saxon-Swedish army under

Gustavus inflicts crushing defeat on Tilly at battle of Breitenfeld. Imperial power in the north broken; Protestant hopes revive. Arnim captures Prague. Gustavus heads for the rich Rhineland.

Treaty of Cherasco ends Mantuan dispute in France's favor.

Wallenstein recalled by Ferdinand.

1632   Gustavus defeats Tilly, who dies shortly thereafter. Swedish troops invade Bavaria. Wallenstein drives Saxons out of Bohemia and then unites with Bavarian troops. He meets Gustavus at battle of Lützen: Swedes win, but Gustavus is killed. Christina Queen of Sweden. Oxenstierna, Chancellor of Sweden, takes over conduct of war.

1633   Confederation of Heilbronn: alliance of German Protestants and Sweden. Swedish army taken over by Bernard of Saxe-Weimar.

Wallenstein negotiates secretly with Saxony, Sweden, and Bohemian exiles.

France occupies Lorraine.

1634   Ferdinand dismisses Wallenstein. Army turns against Wallenstein, who flees to Eger where he is murdered.

Imperial army defeats Swedes at battle of Nördlingen.

1635   Treaty of Prague: Saxony makes peace with Ferdinand. Bavaria, Brandenburg, and most princes of the Empire accept the terms, which offer amnesty to all except the leaders of Bohemian and Palatinate opposition, and make a compromise over the Edict of Restitution.

Richelieu subsidizes Bernard of Saxe-Weimar's army, allies himself with the Dutch and some Italian princes, and then enters the war.

France occupies the Valtelline.

1636   Spanish troops invade France, reach Corbie, within 100 miles of Paris.

Ferdinand has his son elected King of the Romans.

1637   Death of Ferdinand II. Ferdinand III Emperor.

Dutch recapture Breda.

French leave the Valtelline.

1638   Bernard of Saxe-Weimar captures Breisach, important Rhine fortress, for France.

1639   Death of Bernard of Saxe-Weimar. France takes over his army.

Battle of the Downs: defeat of Spanish fleet by the Dutch.

1640   Revolts of Portugal and Catalonia against Spain.

Frederick William becomes Elector of Brandenburg: starts to build up an army that is to give him a powerful position at peace negotiations.

1641   First major discussions of peace at Hamburg. Decision to have a peace congress.

1642   Second battle of Breitenfeld: Swedish victory.

Death of Richelieu: Cardinal Mazarin takes over as chief minister.

1643   War between Denmark and Sweden diverts Swedish army.

Negotiations for peace between Sweden and Emperor begin at Osnabrück (in Westphalia).

Olivares dismissed by Philip IV.

French defeat Spaniards at battle of Rocroi.

Death of Louis XIII. Child Louis XIV King: Regency rule in France under Mazarin.

1644 Battle of Freiburg: defeat of French by Bavaria.

Negotiations for peace between the Emperor and France begin at Münster (in Westphalia).

George Rakoczy leads a new revolt against the Emperor in Hungary with French, Swedish and Dutch support.

1645 Treaty of Brömsebro ends Danish-Swedish war in Sweden's favor.

Second battle of Nördlingen: French and Swedes defeat Bavaria and the Emperor.

Rakoczy defeated and makes peace.

1646 Swedes and French invade Bavaria.

1647 Truce of Ulm: Maximilian of Bavaria agrees to become neutral, but breaks the agreement and rejoins the Emperor.

Revolts in Naples and Sicily against Spanish rule.

1648 Bavaria devastated. Swedes reach Prague.

Treaties signed in Westphalia, giving great gains to France and Sweden.

German princes gain virtual independence; important territorial gains for Bavaria, Saxony, and Brandenburg. The Dutch and Swiss recognized as independent.

Death of Christian IV of Denmark.

Outbreak of the first of a series of revolts (lasting till 1654) in France, known as the Fronde.

1651 Death of Maximilian I of Bavaria.

1655–1660 War between Sweden, Denmark, Brandenburg, Poland, and Russia. Ends with Treaties of Copenhagen, Oliva and Kardis.

1659 Treaty of the Pyrenees ends war between France and Spain, giving France further territorial gains.

NOTE: Accounts which deal with the Thirty Years' War as a self-contained unit (i.e. not as part of some other process, such as the winning of independence by the Dutch) usually subdivide the three decades into distinct phases of conflict. The most common division is into four periods: The Bohemian through 1625, the Danish through 1629, the Swedish through 1635, and the French (and Swedish) through 1648. Despite occasional variations on this traditional schema (Ogg, for instance, treats the first two periods as one—the defeat of Protestantism; Pagès makes a sevenfold division; and Wedgwood has ten separate phases), it continues to provide the basic pattern for nearly all histories of the war.

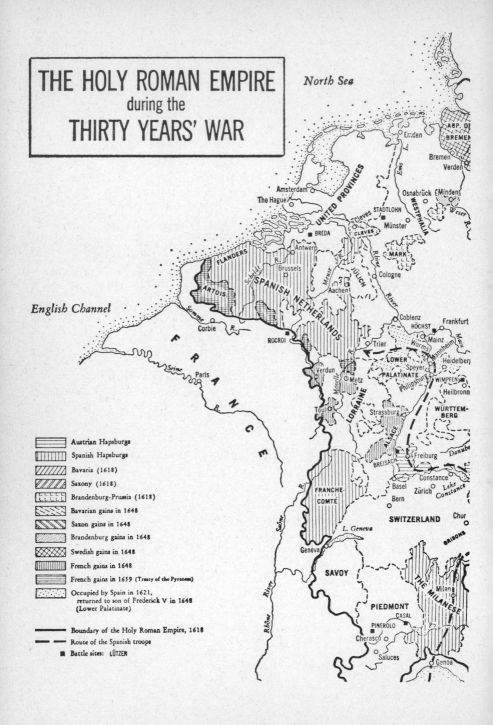

THE HOLY ROMAN EMPIRE
during the
THIRTY YEARS' WAR

North Sea

English Channel

ABP. OF BREMEN
Emden
Bremen
Verden
Amsterdam
The Hague
Osnabrück
Minden
WESTPHALIA
UNITED PROVINCES
Cleves
STADTLOHN
Weser R.
CLEVES
Münster
BREDA
Antwerp
Rhine
MARK
FLANDERS
Brussels
Meuse
JÜLICH
Cologne
Scheldt R.
SPANISH NETHERLANDS
Aachen
ARTOIS
Rhine River
Somme R.
Coblenz
Frankfurt
Corbie R.
HÖCHST
Mainz
ROCROI
Trier
Worms
Mannheim
Main
Verdun
LOWER
Speyer
Heidelberg
Seine
Moselle
PALATINATE
Philipsburg
WIMPFEN
Paris
Metz
Heilbronn
FRANCE
Toul
LORRAINE
Strassburg
WÜRTTEMBERG
ALSACE
Danube
Freiburg
BREISAC
Constance
FRANCHE-
COMTÉ
Basel
Zürich
Lake Constance
Bern
SWITZERLAND
Chur
L. Geneva
Geneva
GRISONS
SAVOY
THE MILANESE
Milan
Seine River
PIEDMONT
CASAL
PINEROLO
Cherasco
Genoa
Rhône River
Saluces

Austrian Hapsburgs
Spanish Hapsburgs
Bavaria (1618)
Saxony (1618)
Brandenburg-Prussia (1618)
Bavarian gains in 1648
Saxon gains in 1648
Brandenburg gains in 1648
Swedish gains in 1648
French gains in 1648
French gains in 1659 (Treaty of the Pyrenees)
Occupied by Spain in 1621,
  returned to son of Frederick V in 1648
  (Lower Palatinate)

——— Boundary of the Holy Roman Empire, 1618
– – – Route of the Spanish troops
■ Battle sites: LÜTZEN

The Conflict of Opinion

On the war

> The opposition between the interests of the house of Hapsburg and of the German nation, and between the old and new faith, led to a bloody catastrophe. . . . When the war ended, there was little remaining of the great nation. . . . That which will here be depicted . . . is a sad and joyless time.
>
> GUSTAV FREYTAG

> It has become customary to call the Thirty Years' War a war of religion. Yet even a fleeting glance at the course of events shows this interpretation to be untenable. . . . [But] the assertion that one must keep religion completely out of the picture . . . is as distorted as the assertion that it was a religious war. Historical materialism does not in any way deny . . . that religious belief played a great role. . . . It asserts only that religion was as little the final cause . . . as any ideology, because only in the field of economics can these causes be sought.
>
> FRANZ MEHRING

> The war was an unmitigated catastrophe. . . . As there was no compulsion towards a conflict which . . . took so long to engage and needed so much assiduous blowing to fan the flame, so no right was vindicated by its ragged end. The war solved no problem. . . . Morally subversive, economically destructive, socially degrading, confused in its causes, devious in its course, futile in its result, it is the outstanding example in European history of meaningless conflict.
>
> C. V. WEDGWOOD

> The series of wars ending with the peace of the Pyrenees (1659) solved the outstanding problem of Europe: the final overthrow of the Hapsburg hegemony established the principle of the balance of power. . . . It is the outstanding example in European history of an intrinsically successful settlement. . . . German affairs were of minor importance. . . . The conception of the Thirty Years' War as a "war of religions" has been abandoned to a large extent since it has been recognized that religious divisions coincided largely with political, constitutional and economic ones. . . . The ruinous effect of the war years . . . has been very much exaggerated. . . . [The] whole system of German economics was breaking down . . . from the middle of the sixteenth century. . . . The big inflation of the years 1619–1623 . . . was the fever which preceded the patient's recovery. . . . On the whole, the national income, productive

power and standard of living were higher about 1650 than they had been fifty years earlier.

S. H. STEINBERG

Steinberg's basic premise that a nadir was reached in 1623 is not supported by the evidence. . . . At best, the Thirty Years' War started a general decline that had not previously existed; at worst, it replaced prosperity with disaster.

THEODORE K. RABB

Thus, it appears that the political conflict, commonly called the Thirty Years' War, was the logical outcome of the crisis of policy of the old feudal ruling class. This political crisis of the declining sixteenth and the commencing seventeenth centuries had deep social and economic roots.

J. V. POLIŠENSKÝ

On Gustavus Adolphus:

The true glory of the King of Sweden was that he was the champion of Protestantism.

C. R. L. FLETCHER

Gustav Adolf was essentially an empirical statesman. He had no grandiose or cut-and-dried political plans. He dealt with situations as they arose, by successive expedients. . . . Security, not empire-building, was his real purpose.

MICHAEL ROBERTS

On Wallenstein:

He always lived in the midst of his grand designs, in which . . . the public interest was mixed up with his private aims, though if we do not misunderstand him, the former predominated.

LEOPOLD VON RANKE

A weakling . . . confused by superstitions, impelled by titanic and megalomanic schemes of revenge, a cowardly traitor, and a foolish intriguer.

JOSEF PEKAŘ

On Richelieu:

Richelieu was eaten up by a consuming lust for power. . . . Everything he did was planned and calculated for the sole purpose of bringing, not indeed the greatest happiness to the greatest number, but the greatest advantage to Armand Du Plessis de Richelieu and the greatest glory to France.

ALDOUS HUXLEY

The decision to open hostilities . . . was imposed by events, and was not the result of a completely free choice by Richelieu. . . . One often finds oneself led to the conclusion that the course of events had more of an effect on his policy than not.

V. L. TAPIÉ

I GENERAL INTERPRETATIONS OF THE CAUSES, NATURE, AND EFFECTS OF THE THIRTY YEARS' WAR

Gustav Freytag

THE GERMAN CATASTROPHE

Gustav Freytag (1816–1895) was a highly successful German novelist and playwright. After studying philology at the Universities of Breslau and Berlin he became an instructor in German language and literature in Breslau. A long list of plays, poems, and novels followed. In 1847 he moved to Berlin, where he became an editor of a leading liberal weekly journal. He made an international reputation with his novel Credit and Debit, *a realistic but favorable portrayal of the German commercial class. His* Pictures out of the German Past, *from which the following selections on the Thirty Years' War are taken, appeared in five volumes between 1859 and 1862, and became an immensely popular version of German history.*

The political [condition] of Germany before the Thirty Years' War [was] most unsatisfactory. . . . Discontent was general, a mournful tendency, a disposition to prophesy evil, were the significant signs of the times. Every deed of violence which was announced to the people in the [news] sheets, was accompanied by remarks on the bad times. And yet we know for certain that immorality had not become strikingly greater in the country. There was wealth in the cities, and even in the country increase of prosperity; there was regular government everywhere, better order and greater security of existence, luxury and an inordinate love of enjoyment had undoubtedly increased, together with riches; even among the lower strata of the people greed was awakened, life became more varied and dearer, and much indifference began to be shown concerning the quarrels of ecclesiastics. The best began to be gloomy, and even cheerful natures . . . became prophets of misfortune, and wished for death.

And there was good reason for this gloom. There was something diseased in the life of Germany, an incomprehensible burden weighed it down, which marred its development. Luther's teaching, it is true, produced the greatest spiritual and intellectual progress which Germany had ever made through one man, but the demands of life increased with every expansion of the soul. The new mental culture must be followed by a corresponding advance in earthly condition, a

From Gustav Freytag, *Pictures of German Life in the XVth, XVIth and XVIIth Centuries,* tr. Georgiana Malcolm (London, 1862), II: 8–11, 14–17.

greater independence in faith, demanded imperiously a stronger power of political development. But it was precisely this teaching, which appeared like the early dawn of a better life, that conveyed to the people the consciousness of their own political weakness, and by this weakness they became one-sided and narrow-minded. Germany being divided into countless territories under weak princes, its people everywhere involved in and occupied with trifling disputes, were deficient in that which is indispensable to a genial growth; they needed a general elevation, a great united will, and a sphere of moral duties, which alone makes men preeminently cheerful and manly. The fatherland of the Germans extended probably from Lorraine to the Oder, but in no single portion of it did they live like the citizens of Elizabeth or Henry IV.

Thus already inwardly diseased, Germany entered upon a war of thirty years. When the war ended, there was little remaining of the great nation. For yet a century to come, the successors of the survivors were deficient in that most manly of all feelings,—political enthusiasm.

Luther had raised his people out of the epic life of the middle ages. The Thirty Years' War had destroyed the popular strength, and forced the Germans into individual life, the mental constitution of which one may truly call lyrical. That which will here be depicted from the accounts of contemporaries, is a sad joyless time.

The opposition between the interests of the house of Hapsburg and of the German nation, and between the old and new faith, led to a bloody catastrophe. If any one should inquire how such a war could rage through a whole generation, and so fearfully exhaust a powerful people, he will receive this striking answer, that the war was so long and terrible, because none of the contending parties were able to carry it out on a great and decisive scale. . . .

It is evident that there was a fatal disproportion between the military strength of the parties and the ultimate object of every war. None of them could entirely subdue their opponents. The armies were too small, and had too little durability, to be able to control by regular strategic operations, the numerous and warlike people of widespread districts. Whilst a victorious army was ruling near the Rhine or the Oder, a new enemy was collecting in the north on the shores of the Baltic. The German theater of war, also, was not so constituted as to be easily productive of lasting results. Almost every city, and many country seats were fortified. The siege guns were still unwieldy and uncertain in their aim, and the defense of fortified places was proportionably stronger than the attack. Thus war became principally a combat of sieges; every captured town weakened the victorious army, from the necessity of leaving garrisons. When a province had been conquered, the conqueror was often not in a position to withstand the conquered in open battle. By new exertion the conqueror was driven from the field; then followed fresh sieges and captures, and again fatal disruption of strength.

It was a war full of bloody battles and glorious victories, and also of excessive alternations of fortune. Numerous were the dark hero forms that loomed out of the chaos of blood and fire; the iron Ernst von Mansfeld, the fantastic Brunswicker, Bernhard of Weimar; and on the other side, Maximilian of Bavaria, and the generals of the League, Tilly, Pappenheim, and the able Mercy; the leaders of the Imperial army, the daring Wallenstein and Altringer; the great French heroes, Condé and Turenne, and amongst the Swedes, Horn, Bauer, Torstenson, Wrangel, and above all the mighty prince of war, Gustavus Adolphus. How much manly energy excited to the highest pitch, and yet how slow and poor were the political results obtained! How quickly was again lost, what appeared to have been obtained by the greatest amount of power! How often did the parties themselves change the objects after which they were striving, nay even the banner for which they desired victory!

The political events of the war can only be briefly mentioned here; they may be divided into three periods. The first, from 1618 to 1630, is the time of the Imperial triumphs. The Protestant estates of Bohomia, contrary to law and their own word, refused the Bohemian crown to the Archduke Ferdinand, and chose for their ruler the Elector Palatine, a reformer. But by means of the League and the Lutheran Electors of Saxony, Ferdinand became Emperor. His opponent was beaten in the battle of the White Mountain, and left the country as a fugitive. Here and there, the Protestant opposition continued to blaze up, but divided without plan, and with weak resources. . . . Ferdinand II, who though Emperor, was still a fugitive in the states belonging to his house, obtained through the assistance of an experienced mercenary commander, Wallenstein, a large body of troops, whom he maintained in the territory of the principality by contribution and pillage. Ever greater did the Emperor's army continue to swell; ever higher rose his claims in Germany and Italy: the old idea of Charles V . . . became a living principle in the nephew; he would subdue Germany, as his predecessor had done the peasants and the estates in the Austrian provinces; he would crush all independence, the privileges of cities, the rights of the estates, the pride and family power of princes—he hoped to subjugate all Germany to his faith and his house. But throughout the whole of Germany sounded a cry of grief and indignation, at the horrible marauding war which was conducted by the merciless general of the Hapsburger. All the allies of the Imperial house rose threateningly against him. The princes of the League, and above all Maximilian of Bavaria, looked abroad for help; they subdued the high spirit of the Emperor, and he was obliged to dismiss his faithful General and to control the barbarous army. Nay, more, even the Holy Father began to fear the Emperor. The Pope himself united with France in order to bring Swedish help to the Protestants. The lion of the north disembarked on the German coast.

Now began the second period of the war. The swelling billows of the Roman Catholic power had overflowed Germany even up to the Northern Sea. From 1630 to 1634 came the Protestant counter-current, which flowed in a resistless course from north to south over the third part of Germany. Even after the death of their king, the Swedish Generals kept their ascendancy in the field; Wallenstein himself abandoned the Emperor, and was secretly murdered. The Roman Catholic party had begun to lose courage, when, by a last effort of collected strength, it won the bloody battle of Nördlingen.

Then followed the third period of fourteen years, from 1634 to 1648, in which victory and reverses were nearly equal on both sides. The Swedes, driven back to the Northern Sea, girding up their whole strength, again burst forth into the middle of Germany. Again the tide of fortune ebbed to and fro, becoming gradually less powerful. The French, greedy of booty, spread themselves as far as the Rhine; the land was devastated, and famine and pestilence raged. The Swedes, though losing one General after another, kept the field and maintained their claims with unceasing pertinacity. In opposition to them stood the equally inflexible Maximilian, prince of the League. Even in the last decade of the war, the Bavarians fought for three years the most renowned campaigns which this dynasty has to boast of. The fanatical Ferdinand was dead, his successsor, able, moderate, and an experienced soldier, persevered from necessity; he also was firm and tenacious. No party could bring about a decisive result. For years negotiations for peace were carried on; while the generals fought, the cities and villages were depopulated and the fields were overgrown with rank weeds. Peace came at last; it was not brought about by great battles, nor by irresistible political combinations, but chiefly by the weariness of the combatants, and Germany celebrated it with festivities though she had lost three fourths of her population.

All this gives to the Thirty Years' War the appearance of foredoomed annihilation, ushered in as it was by the most fearful visitations of nature. Above the strife of parties a terrible fate spread its wings; it carried off the leaders and prostrated them in the dust, the greatest human strength became powerless under its hand; at last, satiated with devastation and death, it turned its face slowly from the country which had become a great charnel house.

Anton Gindely

RELIGION AND POLITICS

Anton Gindely (1829–1892) was a Czech historian who taught first at the University of Olmütz and then became a professor at the University of Prague. Appointed archivist to the kingdom of Bohemia, and with the help of governmental support, he was able to do extensive research in archives throughout central Europe and later as far afield as Spain. One of the founders of modern Czech historiography, he did a great deal of the essential groundwork on which later work has been based. His most important enterprise was the launching of the first major collection of the documents of Bohemian history, whose earliest volumes he edited until his death. Much of his work was on the Thirty Years' War, and his history of the war, from whose opening pages the following selection is taken, was published in 1882.

From Anton Gindely, *History of the Thirty Years' War*, tr. Andrew Ten Brook, Vol. I (New York, 1884), pp. 20–22.

The cause of the murderous war which, for thirty years of the seventeenth century, lacerated central Europe is to be sought chiefly in the incompatibility of the religious views which prevailed among the peoples of the time. The discord, indeed, continues to this day, but utters itself no longer in bloody conflicts. The ground, however, of the pacific disposition which now obtains lies either in general indifference or in spreading skepticism. While Catholics and Protestants maintained their earlier zeal for their faith, their convictions of the truth of their opinions and the errors of their opponents were of a kind which, in our time, we seek in vain, even in men of most rigid beliefs, and which is now exemplified only among the national party leaders of a land where two languages are spoken, and there, only in a milder form. Is it then a matter of wonder that religious conflict then raged more wildly than does now the political, and that satisfaction was found, not in the subjugation, but in the extermination, of the opposing party? It would be unreasonable to ascribe to one of the religious parties alone the guilt of this fierce struggle; they were equally guilty. If, in one land, the one received harder blows than it dealt out, the account was nevertheless balanced in some other. To be just in judging the contending personalities, we may not make the efforts of our own party our rule of fitness for the dispensing of our praise and blame. We should judge them by the ability with which they filled their places and carried out their plans; by the self-sacrificing spirit which actuated them in relation to their associates, and should inquire also whether they observed, and in what manner they observed, those eternal, moral laws which are respected alike by all Christian nations. Led by these principles we can rightly judge such men as Ferdinand II, Maximilian of Bavaria, and Gustavus Adolphus, and do them justice, although their action was so opposite that the approval of the one seems to involve the condemnation of the other.

But disagreement in religious convictions was not the sole cause of the war. The insubordination of the Estates in Austria, the avidity of the princes to enrich themselves at the cost of the Church property, the ambition of individual party leaders, who could be satisfied only in a general disorder, contributed so largely to the kindling of the conflagration as to make it doubtful to what particular the greater guilt should be ascribed. But whatever may have kindled the strife, it is certain that its long duration was caused only by material interests.

Though ideal views may give rise to a war, this once begun, the material questions of possession and power advance to the front and become, in contests which the party at first defeated would have been glad to end by yielding somewhat, the causes of continuance. All the princes and statesmen who came successively to participate in the Thirty Years' War wished to augment their power by triumph. This is true of Ferdinand II and Maximilian of Bavaria; of Louis XIII, and his minister, Cardinal Richelieu; of Gustavus Adolphus and Oxenstiern. Having once drawn the sword, the question was the same with all—increase of territory and people. All the words with which they tried to conceal this purpose were empty phrases, which never deceived those who employed them. We would not, however, deny that Ferdinand II and Gustavus Adolphus, each in his way, regarded themselves as chosen instruments of God, and that their efforts were not, like those of Louis XIII, governed by mere desire of conquest. It is, however, a sad aspect of human life, that no ideal endeavors—the religious any more than the political and national—are fully successful, except in the material ruin of antagonists, and that their representatives, however well disposed, cannot but take into consideration these consequences of success. Such views guide us in the following narrative.

Franz Mehring

THE MARXIST VIEW: ECONOMIC CAUSATION

Franz Mehring (1846–1919) was one of the most prominent German socialists of the late nineteenth and early twentieth centuries. He came from an upper middle-class Pomeranian family, and as a student of philosophy, he became an adherent of Lassalle. However, he withdrew from socialist activities and wrote for various conservative newspapers until 1891, when he returned to socialism, became a member of the Social Democrat party, and rapidly achieved an international reputation as one of its leading left-wing thinkers.

From Franz Mehring, *Zur Deutschen Geschichte* (Berlin, 1931), pp. 265–271, 283, 286 and 318. Editor's Translation.

*He eventually became one of the most outspoken opponents of the 1914–
1918 war, and a founder of the German Communist party. His articles and
books covered subjects from literature and philosophy to history, politics and
militarism. He published a biography of Karl Marx in 1918, and his historical
writings, collected after his death, reveal him to have been a loyal disciple of
Marx. His Marxist views will be evident from the following passages out of an
essay on Gustavus Adolphus which originally appeared in 1894. The essay as
a whole is an excellent, if extreme, example of that branch of German historical writing which takes a hostile view of the Swedish King, portraying him
as a disastrous foreign intruder into German affairs. Mehring's study also
exemplifies the point made in the introduction to this booklet, where it was
noted that a historian's assessment of the leading participants is often the
best indication of his view of the nature of the Thirty Years' War, and vice
versa.*

I

It has become customary to call the Thirty Years' War a war of religion. Yet even a fleeting glance at the course of events shows this
interpretation to be untenable. For Europe the outcome of the war
was the replacement of Spanish supremacy by French, and France
was as much a Catholic power as Spain. The Protestant princes in
Germany accepted the protection of the Catholic King of France and
even that of the Grand Turk in Constantinople. When Gustavus Adolphus stormed into Germany, supposedly to save Protestantism, the
Protestant Netherlands refused to ally with him, but on the other
hand his undertaking had the blessing of the Pope. And one can take
into the dozens the examples of Catholics fighting Catholics, Protestants fighting Protestants, Catholics on the side of Protestants, and
Protestants on the side of Catholics.

To say that religion had nothing to do with the Thirty Years' War,
however, would be to throw the baby out with the bath water. Numerous actions of the combatants are evidence to the contrary. Countless
people went to their deaths in zeal for the Holy Mother of God or the
"pure faith," or some other religious symbol that we no longer understand. However many examples there are of coreligionists fighting
one another, there are also many where religious beliefs divided or
united. England and Holland fought under the Protestant banner
against Catholic Spain, and on the other side the Counter Reformation tied Spain to Austria. The assertion that one must keep religion
completely out of the picture if one is to assess the Thirty Years' War

correctly is as distorted as the assertion that it was a religious war. Historical materialism does not in any way deny, as perfidious or ignorant people have charged, that religious belief played a great role in history. On the contrary, it fully recognizes this motive in historical development. It asserts only that religion was as little the final cause of such development as any ideology, because only in the field of economics can these causes be sought.

With this guide one can then also find one's way out of the hopeless jumble of contrary opinions that is encountered by anyone who tries to assess the Thirty Years' War by taking the religious point of view into consideration either exclusively or not at all. According to Marx, one must distinguish between the material revolution in the economic conditions of production and the ideological forms through which people become aware of this conflict and fight it out. These forms in the seventeenth century were predominantly religious, no longer as strongly religious as in the sixteenth century, but much more strongly religious than in the eighteenth century, at the conclusion of which the French Revolution for the first time threw off the cloak of religion and appeared in purely worldly forms of thought. But if one asks why, between the sixteenth and eighteenth centuries, awareness of material conflicts by the classes and people of Europe took religious forms, the answer is that the Christian Church had saved the remains of ancient culture for these classes and people after the collapse of the Roman Empire, that it had led the entire material life of the European West for a thousand years, and that consequently it had also completely permeated this life with a religious spirit.

The medieval Church was an economic power in religious forms. This power had to collapse as soon as its particular conditions of production, feudalism, collapsed. Feudal conditions of production collapsed all the more helplessly the faster capitalistic methods of production grew. . . . A tremendous revolution in the methods of production changed completely the attitude of the people of Europe toward the medieval Church. Instead of a support for the feudal economy, this Church became a hindrance to capitalistic production, . . . but . . . it held on all the more stubbornly to its old power. . . . A break with the papacy became inevitable.

This break with an economic power that ruled through religious forms could be achieved only by economic resistance that also took religious forms. . . . The further capitalism developed, and with it the understanding of society and nature, the more the secrets of the life processes of society and nature were revealed, and the roots of all religion thus withered away. But these roots received new life . . . when . . . the people could find no other way to explain this revolution . . . than as a judgment of supernatural powers. The result was a dismal and dreadful fanaticism that . . . seemed to turn Western Europe into a madhouse which, in the Thirty Years' War, was being set on fire on all sides by its deranged inmates. Nevertheless, this fanaticism was bound to disappear in the long run as capitalistic methods of production developed. At the time of the Thirty Years' War it was more or less clear to the ruling classes that the world was governed by economic facts and not by their religious reflections. . . .

The three great religious streams in the first half of the seventeenth century consisted of Jesuits, Calvinists and Lutherans. All three formed new Churches which differed from the old Church as capitalistic differed from feudal methods of production. . . . For the differences between these religions to lead to a thirty year war, to decimate flourishing lands, to slaughter millions upon millions of people, would seem possible only in a lunatic asylum. Yet behind these differences stood the economic conflicts of the Europe of that period.

The Jesuits represented Catholicism reformed on a capitalistic basis. . . . As opposed to the absolutist-capitalistic Society of Jesus, one can call Calvinism the townsman-capitalistic religion . . . [and] Lutheranism the religion of economically backward lands. . . .

[The peace of Augsburg] had a large loophole. It put the seal on the plunder of Church lands accomplished up to that time by the Protestant princes, but what was to be done henceforth with the many Church territories that remained in Germany? The Lutherans claimed that in these territories the principle *cujus regio, ejus religio* should not apply—their Lutheran inhabitants should be permitted to follow their beliefs unmolested. The Catholics on the other hand wanted the same terms for spiritual princes as for secular princes. This was one difference of opinion that was not resolved. The second consisted of the so-called "spiritual restriction" claimed by the Catholic side. According to this, every spiritual prince, elector, archbishop, bishop or abbot who deserted to the "pure teaching" would be deprived of his spiritual offices and positions. The Lutheran princes, however, wanted to have none of this because it would have deprived them of the most convenient method of acquiring Church property. . . . With both of these open questions there was created in the religious Peace of Augsburg the great loophole through which the Thirty Years' War was to come. . . .

Under the guise of religious peace new sources of unrest multiplied rapidly. Very worldly power interests fought under cover of religion. In the year 1607 the pious Duke Max of Bavaria took some kind of religious squabble as the pretext to grab the free imperial city of Donauwörth by the throat and to stick it into his knapsack. This daring show of force gave the first signal for the mobilization of the armies. Some of the Protestant princes allied themselves under the Union, led by the Palatinate, at which the Catholic princes joined together in the League led by Bavaria. . . . In this situation began . . . the . . . period of . . . the Thirty Years' War. . . .

II

No work of history has yet calculated what, according to the existing and critically examined sources, the Thirty Years' War cost the German people in all instances. Only one thing is certain beyond any doubt: never has a great civilized nation had to endure comparable destruction. According to the most reliable estimates, more than three quarters of the population was annihilated—during the thirty years the total sank from seventeen to four million. The decimation of economic life on all sides was of similar proportions. Germany's development was thrown back two hundred years. It took two hundred years to reach again the economic level that had been achieved at the beginning of the Thirty Years' War. With all its limbs mutilated, the German monarchy was no more than a moldering corpse. It was relatively of small account that the Netherlands and Switzerland were torn away from their last, loose ties with the Empire. In the west, France grabbed the richest areas for herself, in the north, Sweden plundered the mouths of the Oder, the Elbe and the Weser, and both nations kept the right to interfere in German affairs. The last authority of the Emperor and the Empire was irretrievably lost. In the shattered Edict of Restitution the House of Hapsburg got the requital it deserved for its

A la fin ces Voleurs infames et perdus,
Comme fruits malheureux a cet arbre pendus

Monstrent bien que le crime (horrible et noire engeance)
Est luy mesme instrument de honte et de vengeance,

Et que c'est le Destin des hommes vicieux
Desprouuer tost ou tard la iustice des Cieux. 1)

Israel ex. Cum Priuil. Reg.

FIGURE 1. *The Hanging*, by Jacques Callot (1592–1635). Callot was one of the greatest masters of the art of etching in the seventeenth century, and received a number of commissions from princes who wanted representations of heroic moments in battle. Near the end of his life, however, he became deeply unhappy about the effects of warfare that raged about him, and in 1633 he produced two magnificent series of etchings entitled *The Miseries of War*. *The Hanging*, his most famous, depicts a mass execution of looters, surrounded by the panoply of war and religion (note the priest on the ladder), a scene almost certainly inspired by a real incident, for Callot had just spent a number of months observing the war in the Netherlands. *(Courtesy of the Art Museum, Princeton University)*

suicidal policy. The economic causes of the German Reformation continued to operate; the "liberty of the Estates" triumphed all the way along the line. The absolute sovereignty of the princes, which included the right to make foreign alliances, also gave the German people at last the happy assurance that, after all the terrible suffering, after all the boundless ignominy, the cup of suffering and ignominy was still far from completely drained.

C. V. Wedgwood
THE FUTILE AND MEANINGLESS WAR

C. V. Wedgwood is one of the most prolific English historians of the day and a leading authority on the seventeenth century. Born in Northumberland, she has studied in France, Germany and at Oxford. Her first book, on the Earl of Strafford, appeared in 1935, and since that time she has published studies of Oliver Cromwell, William the Silent, Richelieu, Montrose, and a revision of her Strafford in the light of new evidence—a rarity among historical works. She has also written numerous essays and is now in the midst of a history of the English Civil War, a number of whose volumes have appeared. Her history of the Thirty Years War appeared in 1938, and, as she herself admits, "the preoccupations of that unhappy time cast their shadows over its pages. . . . Preoccupation with contemporary distress made the plight of the hungry and homeless, the discouraged and the desolate in the Thirty Years War exceptionally vivid to me. . . . The atmosphere of the nineteen thirties had something to do with my choice of subject as well as with my methods of treatment. Many of my generation who grew up under the shadow of the First World War had a sincere, if mistaken, conviction that all wars were unnecessary and useless."

I

The year 1618 was like many others in those uneasy decades of armed neutrality which occur from time to time in the history of Europe.

From C. V. Wedgwood, *The Thirty Years War* (London, 1938). This selection has been taken from the Doubleday paperback edition (New York, 1961), pp. 11, 13, 20, 22–23, 26–28, 32–37, 40–41, 44–47, 50–53, 505–506 and 7–8. Reprinted by permission of Jonathan Cape Limited.

Political disturbances exploded intermittently in an atmosphere thick with the apprehension of conflict. Diplomatists hesitated, weighing the gravity of each new crisis, politicians predicted, merchants complained of unsteady markets and wavering exchanges, while the forty million peasants, on whom the cumbrous structure of civilization rested, dug their fields and bound their sheaves and cared nothing for the remote activities of their rulers.

In London the Spanish ambassador demanded the life of Sir Walter Raleigh while the people, crowding about the palace, shouted imprecations at a King too weak to save him. In The Hague the rivalry of two religious factions broke again and again into open riot, and the widow of William the Silent was hissed in the streets. Between France and Spain relations were strained to the uttermost, each government claiming control of the Val Telline, the key pass between Italy and Austria. In Paris they feared immediate rupture and European war; in Madrid they doubted whether the recent marriage of the Infanta Anne to the young King of France would withstand the strain. At seventeen, Louis XIII treated his wife's advances with an icy indifference, so that the dissolution of an unconsummated marriage might at any moment remove the last guarantee of friendship between the ruling dynasties of France and Spain. In vain the Austrian cousins of the Spanish King intervened from Vienna with the tentative offer of a young Archduke for a French princess; the regency government in Paris, disregarding the suggestion, opened negotiations for a marriage with the eldest son of the Duke of Savoy, the avowed enemy both of the Austrian and the Spanish rulers.

The discovery of a Spanish plot to overthrow the republican government of Venice and a rising of the Protestants in the Val Telline threatened to submerge Italy in war. In northern Europe the ambitious King of Sweden secured Esthonia and Livonia from the Tsar of Russia, and projected a firm alliance with the Dutch which, had it succeeded, would have established their joint control over the northern waters of Europe. In Prague an unpopular Catholic government was overthrown by a well-timed Protestant rising.

The political world was in a state of nervous exasperation acute enough to invest any one of these incidents with an exaggerated importance. The probability of war was a commonplace among the well-informed who doubted only the immediate cause and scope of the conflict; the material and moral antagonisms which divided political life were clear.

May 23rd 1618 was the date of the revolt in Prague; it is the date traditionally assigned to the outbreak of the Thirty Years War. But it was not clear until seventeen months later, even to the leading men in the countries most deeply concerned, that this revolt rather than any other incident in that stormy time had lighted the fire. During the intervening months the affairs of Bohemia became slowly identified with the problems of the European situation. That situation itself brought forth the war. . . .

The generation which preceded the Thirty Years War may not have been more virtuous than its predecessors, but it was certainly more devout. The reaction from the materialism of the Renaissance which had begun towards the middle of the previous century had now reached its widest limits; the spiritual revival had penetrated to the very roots of society and religion was a reality among those to whom politics were meaningless and public events unknown.

Theological controversy became the habitual reading of all classes, sermons directed their politics and moral tracts beguiled their leisure. Among the Catholics the cult of the Saints reached proportions unheard of for centuries and assumed a dominant part in the experience of the educated as well as of the masses; miracles once again made the life of everyday bright with hope. The changes of the material world, the breakdown of old tradition and the insufficiency of dying conventions drove men and women to the spiritual and the inexplicable. Those whom the wide arms of the Churches could not receive took refuge in the occult: Rosicrucianism had crept from Germany to France, Illuminism was gaining hold in Spain. Fear of witchcraft grew among the educated and devil-worship spread among the populace. Black magic was practiced from the desolate north of Scotland to the Mediterranean islands, holding the fierce Celts, the oppressed peasants of Russia, Poland, Bohemia in vengeful terror, no less than sensible merchants of Germany and stolid yeomen of Kent.

Superstitious beliefs were fostered by a pamphlet literature in which every strange happening was immediately recorded and magnified. Gruesome fears lingered even among the educated. . . . Men wanted certainties, not more causes for doubt, and since the discoveries of science perplexed them with strange theories about the earth on which they walked and the bodies they inhabited, they turned with all the more zeal to the firm assurances of religion.

Never had the Churches seemed stronger than in the opening decades of the seventeenth century. Yet a single generation was to witness their deposition from political dominance. The collapse was implicit in the situation of 1618. The fundamental issue was between revealed and rationalized belief, but the sense of danger was not strong enough to bring the Churches together. The lesser issue between Catholic and Protestant obscured the greater, and the Churches had already set the scene for their own destruction.

Superficially there seemed to be two religions in Europe, the Catholic and the Protestant, but in fact the latter was so clearly divided against itself that there were three hostile parties. The Reformation had had two outstanding leaders, Luther and Calvin, and was divided by their teaching, or more exactly by the political consequences of their teaching, into two successive and far from complementary movements. An emotional rather than an intellectual man, Luther had easily fallen a victim to the ambitions of the governing classes: secular rulers had welcomed his teaching because it freed them from the interference of a foreign Pope, and the young movement, too weak to stand on its own feet, had become the servant of the State. Its spiritual force was not destroyed but was at least partly stifled by its material power, and the new Church flourished in the wealth and respectability of its members, grew because kings protected it and merchants approved. This is not to condemn Lutheranism, for men follow their own interests for the highest as well as for the lowest causes, and neither princes nor people accepted Lutheranism in the blandly cynical spirit which a later analysis of their motives might seem to reveal. They believed, doubtless, because they wanted to believe, but the stress in their own minds was on belief, not on desire. Some at least of them died for their faith.

Moreover, the initial defiance of the Pope did not altogether lose its significance because it was so immediately adapted by the secular powers to serve their age-old quarrel with spiritual authority. If the reformed Church gave little encouragement to rebels once it was entrenched behind the State, it had at least shattered the unity of

Catholic Christendom and made way for the exercise of a freer judgement. . . .

In the first years of the Reformation the weakness of Catholic rulers had forced many of them to make concessions to their Protestant subjects, so that, officially at least, there were more Protestant communities in Catholic countries than there were Catholics in Protestant ones. Apart from Italy and Spain, almost all Catholic states tolerated some sort of a Protestant community in their midst. This fact undoubtedly increased the sense of injustice and danger among the Catholic party, just as the slightest infringement of Protestant privilege sent a tremor of indignation through the officially Protestant governments.

The possibility of a clash was constantly present. On the face of it Catholicism, as the older and the more united faith, should have emerged victorious from the conflict. Barely a century had passed since the Reformation, and the Catholic Church cherished the far from illusory hope of reuniting Christendom. The attempt failed. No single cause can explain that failure, yet one stands out above all others. The fortune of the Church became fatally interwoven with that of the House of Austria, and the territorial jealousy evoked by that dynasty reacted upon the Catholic Church by dividing those who should have been her defenders.

In 1618 the Hapsburg dynasty was the greatest power in Europe. "Austriae est imperatura orbi universo" ran their proud device, nor within the narrow limits of the world as conceived by the average European was the boast unfounded. They owned Austria and Tyrol, Styria, Carinthia, Carniola, all Hungary that was not in the hands of the Turk, Silesia, Moravia, Lusatia, and Bohemia; farther west Burgundy, the Low Countries and parts of Alsace; in Italy the duchy of Milan, the fiefs of Finale and Piombino, the kingdom of Naples which covered the whole southern half of the peninsula with Sicily and Sardinia. They were Kings in Spain and Portugal and reigned in the New World over Chile, Peru, Brazil and Mexico. A policy of marriage rather than conquest, they boasted, had made them great, but when heiresses were not to be had they strengthened the solidarity of the dynasty by marriages among themselves; it happened that one prince would be brother-in-law and son-in-law and cousin to another, thrice bound to him in love and duty.

The spectacle of so much concentrated power alone might have roused the envy of neighboring princes, but in the half-century preceding 1618 the dynasty had given warrant for the enmity of its rivals by identifying its policy with two ideas. Its princes stood forth without compromise for absolutism and the Catholic Church and had so relentlessly pursued these convictions that the outside world no longer distinguished between the men and their actions.

The head of the family was the King of Spain, the representative of the elder line; their policy was therefore identified with the militant right wing of Catholicism, that of Saint Ignatius and the Jesuits. The subjection of the family's interests to those of the Spanish King flung into relief one of the oldest feuds in Europe. The rulers of France and Spain had been rivals for the last three centuries: now that the King of Spain was head of a dynasty which controlled most of Italy, the Upper Rhine and the Low Countries, France was threatened on all the landward frontiers. For the last quarter of the sixteenth century the King of Spain had piled fuel on the fire by persistent interference in the internal politics of his neighbor in order to gain control of the Crown itself. He failed, and there emerged triumphant from the conflict the founder of a new French dynasty, the Bourbon, Henry of Navarre. His murder in 1610, at the moment when he had been ready to continue the contest, left his country to a regency too feeble to carry out his projects. Peace was made with Spain and the boy-king married to a Spanish princess. The temporary and deceptive friendship veiled but did not alter the latent enmity of Bourbon and Hapsburg. It remained the most important underlying factor in the European situation.

The immediate problem was the Dutch revolt. The so-called United Provinces, the Protestant northern Netherlands, had rebelled successfully against Philip II; after forty years of fighting they signed a truce with his successor in 1609 by which they gained independence and immunity from attack for twelve years. But the provinces were too valuable to be lightly relinquished, and the Spanish government had granted the long armistice not as a prelude to peace but to give itself leisure to prepare the final reduction of the rebels. The end of the truce in 1621 would precipitate a European crisis—the opportunity for all Protestant rulers to defend a free republic from extinction, or the occasion for the Hapsburg dynasty and the Catholic Church to make a triumphant advance.

The concealed enmity of Bourbon and Hapsburg, the imminent attack of the King of Spain on the Dutch—these dominated the actions of European statesmen in 1618. . . .

By 1618, France had recovered from the devastations of the religious wars and had a rich export trade in wine and corn to England, Germany, Italy and Spain; the southern ports competed with Venice and Genoa in the Levantine trade and the country was becoming the European mart for sugar, silks and spices. As the royal revenues on import and export duties rose, the power of the Crown increased. On the other hand, the trading and farming population grew less tractable with prosperity and the landed nobility were critical and restive. Meanwhile the large and privileged Protestant minority resented the Catholicism of the royal government and encouraged the interference of foreign powers. To this ever-present internal danger was added the further external danger, that Spanish and Austrian agents tampered perpetually with the rulers of the border states of Savoy and Lorraine, both vantage points whence an attack could be made on France.

The French government had one important potential ally. As head of Catholic Christendom the Pope should have rejoiced at the Crusading policy of the Hapsburg dynasty, but as an Italian prince he feared the growth of their power both in the peninsula and throughout Europe. It was therefore natural that he should favor their rivals. The jealousy of the two leading Catholic powers cut clean across the religious alignment of Europe and the highest mission of the Pope should have been to reconcile their quarrel and unite the Catholic world within itself. He lacked both the spiritual authority and the political means; the Vatican moved steadily away from the Hapsburg and towards the Bourbon.

Intermittently, too, the French government commanded the alliance of the Duke of Savoy and the republic of Venice. Both were important. The Duke of Savoy commanded the Alpine passes from France into Italy and was for this reason assiduously wooed by both Hapsburg and Bourbon. His inclination bound him to the latter whenever his timidity did not force him to yield to the former. On the other hand, the territories of the republic of Venice bordered the Val Telline for thirty miles; this valley was the essential pivot of the whole Hapsburg Empire. It was the passage through which convoys of men and money from northern Italy reached the upper waters of the Rhine and Inn, thence to descend either to Austria or the Netherlands. The structure of the Hapsburg Empire was cemented by Spanish money and supported by Spanish troops. Block the Val Telline and the house would fall. Small wonder therefore that the republic of Venice could assert herself with effect against the dynasty; small wonder that the Archduke of Styria and the King of Spain both sought means to overthrow her before she could overthrow them.

The Spaniards aimed to control the Val Telline single-handed but could not afford to offend the Swiss Confederation, one of whose cantons, the Grisons or Grey Leagues, bounded the valley on the northern side. They contented themselves therefore with forming a party in the Grisons, an example instantly followed by the French. The weakest point in the Hapsburg defenses was this one valley, and its possession was to play a part in the politics of the next twenty years out of all proportion to any intrinsic merit which it boasted.

From Spain to Poland, from France to the eastern confines of Swedish Finland and the ice-bound ports of the Baltic, the arch of European politics rested on the keystone of Germany. That immense conglomerate of interdependent states which went by the name of the Holy Roman Empire of the German Nation formed both the geographical and the political center of Europe. In the contest between Hapsburg and Bourbon, between the King of Spain and the Dutch, between Catholics and Protestants, the part that Germany played would be decisive. Every government had realized this and each had tried to establish an interest in that much-divided country.

The Spanish King wanted the Rhine so that his troops and money could be easily transported from north Italy to the Netherlands. The King of France, and the Dutch no less, wanted allies on the Rhine to stop this. The Kings of Sweden and Denmark each sought allies against the other on the Baltic coast, against the King of Poland or against the Dutch. The Pope attempted to form a Catholic party in Germany opposed to the Hapsburg Emperor, the Duke of Savoy intrigued to be elected to the imperial throne.

From Rome, Milan, Warsaw, Madrid, Brussels and The Hague,

Paris, London, Stockholm, Copenhagen, Turin, Venice, Bern, Zurich and Chur, attention was focused on the Empire. The larger issue was that between the dynasties of Hapsburg and Bourbon: the conflict immediately expected was that between the King of Spain and the Dutch republicans. But it was a revolt in Prague and the action of a prince on the Rhine which precipitated the war. The geography and politics of Germany alone give the key to the problem.

Germany's disaster was in the first place one of geography, in the second place one of tradition. From remote times she had been a highway rather than an enclosure, the marching ground of tribes and armies, and when at last the tides of movement ceased, the traders of Europe continued the ancient custom.

Germany was a network of roads knotted together at the intersections by the great clearing-houses at Frankfurt on the Main, Frankfurt on the Oder, Leipzig, Nuremberg, Augsburg. West Indian sugar reached Europe from the refineries of Hamburg, Russian furs from Leipzig, salt fish from Lübeck, oriental silk and spices from Venice through Augsburg, copper, salt, iron, sandstone, corn were carried down the Elbe and Oder, Spanish and English wool woven in Germany competed with Spanish and English cloth in the European market, and the wood that built the Armada was shipped from Danzig. The continual passage of merchants, the going and coming of strangers had more powerfully affected German development than any other single cause. Commerce was her existence, and her cities were more thickly spread than those of any country in Europe. German civilization centered in the small town, but the activities of her traders, the concourse of foreigners to the fairs at Leipzig and Frankfurt, drew the interests of the Germans outwards and away from their own country.

The political traditions of Germany emphasized the development which had originated in a geographical chance. The revival of the Roman Empire by Charlemagne was not wholly fantastic, since he held lands on both sides of the Rhine and the Alps, but when the title passed in time to a line of Saxon kings holding relatively little land in France and Italy the term "Roman Empire" exerted a distorting influence. Classical and medieval ideas, theories and facts in conflict, gave birth about the fifteenth century to the almost apologetic modification of the term "Holy Roman Empire" by the additional phrase "of the German Nation." It was already too late; classical tradition and lust for power attracted the German rulers to campaigns of conquest in Italy, and the German nation was from the outset fatally submerged in the Holy Roman Empire.

Pursuing the shadow of a universal power the German rulers forfeited the chance of a national one. German feudalism, instead of becoming absorbed in the centralized state, disintegrated utterly. Custom and the weakness of the central government increased the self-reliance of each small unit at the expense of the whole until one Emperor declared with blasphemous humor that he was indeed a "King of Kings." Foreign rulers held fiefs within the Empire—the King of Denmark was Duke of Holstein, and the great and scattered estates which made up that whole section of the Empire known as the Burgundian Circle were virtually independent under the King of Spain. Direct vassals of the Emperor, such as the Elector of Brandenburg, held lands outside the Empire and independent of imperial authority. The system had long ceased to conform to any known definition of the state.

The long succession of the Hapsburg to the imperial throne had gravely intensified the danger. Powerful in their hereditary lands they intimidated, but did not control, the lesser princes, who in return opposed all efforts at centralization because they came from a dynasty already too strong. The connection between the Spanish and imperial families was the final disaster, for the Emperor appealed to the King of Spain for help against those who defied his authority, and the princes retaliated by appealing to the enemies of Spain, above all to the King of France. Little by little the German princes laid their country open as a battlefield for foreign rivals. . . .

The mechanism of imperial government could not control the situation. . . . The imperial constitution defied codification. At every election therefore an oath was administered to the Emperor in which the privileges of his subjects were tediously recapitulated. He had to undertake to rule only with the consent of the Diet, to appoint no foreigners to imperial offices, to declare no war and to outlaw none of his subjects by pronouncing the imperial ban against him without the general agreement. This oath or Capitulation varied slightly at every fresh election, and precedent could be found for breaking many if not all of its provisions. Imperial power rested ultimately not on the constitution but on force.

The imperial army was raised by demanding contingents from the separate states and paying for them with money voted in the Diet. The subsidies were confusingly styled "Roman months"—an amount of a hundred and twenty-eight thousand gulden or the sum which the army was supposed to cost for a month. But in the clash of arms which invariably formed the last act of a dispute about imperial authority the Emperor would probably be unable to raise an army at all except through his own private resources. The resources of the Hapsburg dynasty being greater than those of any of their predecessors they had maintained their position comparatively well.

Empty as was the imperial title in 1618, the dynasty had not abandoned the hope of restoring to it the reality of power. With a people as traditional as the Germans a lurking respect for the person of the Emperor was always to be found even among the most rabid exponents of the "German Liberties"—a feeling which an intelligent Emperor could often exploit.

"The German Liberties" was a phrase which had become popular in the sixteenth century. It stood in theory for the constitutional rights of the individual rulers of the Empire, in fact for anything which the caprice or interest of the princes dictated, a bald truth which does not derogate from the personal sincerity with which most of them believed in their own motives. In the smaller group of authoritarians which centered about the Emperor, the corresponding rallying cry was "Justice"; the emphasis was on government here, on independence there. Ultimately there must come a breaking-point. . . .

If it was hard to form two parties on the question of imperial reform when so many currents ran against the main stream of princely interest, religious division made it finally impossible.

A common faith had alone given unity to the disintegrating Empire. When Protestantism rent the confederate principalities asunder, when the more adventurous princes seized upon it as an additional weapon against the Emperor, the theories of five hundred years went up in smoke. At the religious settlement of Augsburg in 1555 the principle of *cujus regio ejus religio* was formulated, by which every prince was permitted to enforce either the Catholic or the Lutheran faith in his lands so that subjects who could not conform must emigrate. This extraordinary compromise saved the theory of religious unity for each state while destroying it for the Empire.

So far the divisions between princes and Empire might have been made the clearer by the religious difference, for the Hapsburg family held by the Catholic faith and were not popular with their Protestant subjects, while the seizure of many bishoprics by the Lutherans in north Germany increased the territorial power of the princes. But Calvinism, appearing within a decade of the settlement, destroyed all chance of a clean issue.

"The Calvinist dragon," declared a Lutheran writer, "is pregnant with all the horrors of Mohammedanism." The frantic fervor with which certain of the German rulers adopted and propagated the new cult gave some justification for the statement. The Elector Palatine in particular demonstrated his disbelief in transubstantiation in the crudest manner. Loudly jeering, he tore the Host in pieces, "What a fine God you are ! You think you are stronger than I? We shall see!" In his austerely whitewashed conventicles a tin basin served for a font and each communicant was provided with his own wooden mug. . . .

The Lutherans were doubly shocked. Although they no longer revered the symbols of the ancient faith, they had preserved them respectfully as the outward signs of their worship and they had a natural esteem for the settlement which had guaranteed them their liberty. They feared that the Calvinists would discredit the whole Protestant movement and they were panic-stricken when, in direct contravention to the settlement of Augsburg, the Calvinists began to proselytize with ruthless thoroughness. The principle of *cujus regio ejus religio* was subject to one reasonable modification. No ruling prelate, abbot, bishop or archbishop, might retain his lands if he should at any time be converted to the Protestant religion. This important rule, the Ecclesiastical Reservation, was as little respected by the Calvinists as the settlement of Augsburg itself, the terms of which had made no provision for any Protestant belief other than the Lutheran.

The Lutherans now began to fear the subversion of that very settlement by right of which they existed. The disregard of imperial edicts by a party who declared that all who were not with them were against them, threatened the Lutherans no less than the Catholics, and among the princes of both these religions there were stumbling gestures towards friendship. Between the uncompromising Catholics on the one side and the Calvinists on the other, a center party was emerging.

There was one element common to the Catholic, Lutheran, and Calvinist religions; each was used by the prince as a means of enforcing his authority. This was well enough for the Hapsburg who held in all their dealings unerringly to the absolutist principle; but for princes who were clamoring for liberties it was a blatant contradiction. They were demanding from the Emperor what they refused to their own people. The libertarian movements, the convulsive outbursts of mercantile or peasant insurrection, terrified those unhappy rulers who were perched between rebellion beneath and oppression above. Two battles were being fought, one between princes and Emperor, another between princes and peoples, and the princes bore the brunt in both, facing both ways, carrying the torch of liberty in one hand and the tyrant's sword in the other.

Unconsciously the natural alliance between those who demanded liberty of conscience and those who demanded political freedom was broken asunder. The religious policy of the reformed princes perverted the natural issue and obscured without destroying the antagonism between the Catholic authoritarian states and their Protestant opponents. The Catholic powers gained. Their position remained clear while that of the Protestants, Calvinists and Lutherans alike, was self-contradictory. . . .

The energy of the educated was perverted into the writing of scurrilous books, which were joyfully received by an undiscriminating public. The Calvinists exhorted all true believers to violence and took special delight in the more blood-thirsty psalms. But the Catholics and Lutherans were not innocent and force was everywhere the proof of true faith. The Lutherans set upon the Calvinists in the streets of Berlin; Catholic priests in Bavaria carried firearms in self-defense; in Dresden the mob stopped the funeral of an Italian Catholic and tore the corpse to pieces; a Protestant pastor and a Catholic priest came to blows in the streets of Frankfurt on the Main, and Calvinist services in Styria were frequently interrupted by Jesuits disguised among the congregation who would tweak the prayer book from the hands of the worshipper and deftly substitute a breviary.

Such things did not happen every day or everywhere. There were years of comparative quiet; there were undisturbed districts; there was marrying and giving in marriage between the three religions; there was friendship and peaceful discussion. But there was no security. . . .

The conditions which had produced Germany's greatness were ceasing to exist. Her culture had rested on the towns: but the towns were declining. The uncertainty of transport in a politically disturbed country and the decline of Italian commerce had disastrously affected German trade. Besides which, her currency was wholly unreliable; there was no effective central authority to control the issues from the countless local mints; princes, towns, and prelates made what profit they chose. . . .

Swedish, Dutch and Danish competition was all this while choking the Hanseatic League, and in all Germany only at Hamburg and at Frankfurt on the Main were there signs of stable and progressive prosperity.

The decline of agriculture was even graver than that of the cities. After the Peasants War, mutual fear between the peasant and the landowner had altogether replaced the old sense of mutual obligation. Landowners grasped every opportunity to increase their power, and serfdom was either stationary or increasing. . . .

Poverty, political unrest, religious divisions, conflicting interests and individual jealousies—these were tinder for a war. Fire was not lacking.

In 1608[1] a riot between Catholics and Protestants at Donauwörth, a free city on the Danube, kept the Empire for some months on the edge of disaster. The Reichshofrat, with imperial approval, divested Donauwörth of its rights and restored its church, wrongfully appropriated by the Protestants, to the Catholics. A storm of indignation from Protestant Germany met this decree and had any leader been forthcoming war must have ensued. But the dispute grew cold among the bickerings of parties, for the cities would not side with the princes nor the Lutherans with the Calvinists.

In 1609 an insurrection in Bohemia forced the Emperor to guarantee religious freedom in that country, but beyond weakening imperial prestige the incident had no immediate results.

[1] Should be 1606.—Ed.

In 1610 the death of the Duke of Cleves-Jülich without heirs brought the third and worst crisis. His lands, the provinces of Jülich, Cleves, Mark, Berg and Ravensberg, formed a scattered group on the Rhine from the Dutch frontier to Cologne and were an essential military base either for the Hapsburg or their opponents. Two claimants, both Protestants, presented themselves, and the Emperor immediately occupied the district with his own troops pending a decision. In order to prevent a serious clash between the rivals the Emperor could hardly have done less, but the Protestant princes interpreted his actions as an attempt to lay hold of the lands for his own dynasty, and Henry IV of France surmised that the King of Spain, anxious to secure this valuable district for his operations against the Dutch, had prompted the Emperor. Henry did not hesitate; acting in alliance with a group of German allies he made ready to invade, and only the chance of his murder averted European war. The leader gone, the controversy dragged from negotiation to negotiation until one of the claimants tried to solve the problem by becoming a Catholic. His rival, the Elector of Brandenburg, in the hope of gaining the support of the extreme Protestant party, became a Calvinist, but the step involved him in so many private difficulties that he was forced in the end to acquiesce in a temporary settlement which gave Jülich and Berg to his rival and left him only Cleves, Mark and Ravensberg.

As the Empire was flung from crisis to crisis, each time righting itself with more difficulty, individual rulers sought their own safety. Strong defenses seemed essential, and a traveler in 1610 was amazed at the threatening show of arms in even the smallest cities. An English tourist, who had been rapidly and roughly ejected from the precincts of a ducal palace, indignantly averred that "these inferior Princes' houses are guarded with hungry halberdiers and reverent musty billmen with a brace or two of hot shots so that their palaces are more like prisons than the free and noble courts of commanding potentates." Arms were supplemented by alliances until the bristling network of hostility was such that the ablest statesman living could not have told where the break would ultimately come and what groups would stand on either side. Solomon himself, said the Emperor's chief adviser, could not have solved the problem of Germany; inside and outside the Empire every diplomatist held his own views and acted on them, waiting for the inevitable explosion.

As the second decade of the century drew to its close and the Empire continued to drift hazardously between the reefs, the conviction became general in Europe that the end of the Dutch truce in 1621 would be the signal for war in Germany. . . . At Vienna the Emperor or Matthias tottered towards the grave. Dreadful things would happen when he was gone, he gloomily predicted. But he had not even the barren contentment of dying in time. In common with Europe he miscalculated the crisis by three years. The signal for war was given not by the end of the Dutch truce in April 1621, but in May 1618, by revolt in Bohemia. . . .

II

In Germany the war was an unmitigated catastrophe. In Europe it was equally, although in a different way, catastrophic. The peace, which had settled the disputes of Germany with comparative success because passions had cooled, was totally ineffectual in settling the problems of Europe. The inconclusive and highly unpopular cession of Alsace led direct to war; the seizure of half Pomerania by the Swedish Crown was only less disastrous because the Swedish Crown was palpably too weak to hold it. The insidious growth of Bourbon influence on the Rhine, and Mazarin's deliberate policy of seizing good strategic points on the frontier, vitiated the settlement. The Peace of Westphalia was like most peace treaties, a rearrangement of the European map ready for the next war.

The Peace has been described as marking an epoch in European history, and it is commonly taken to do so. It is supposed to divide the period of religious wars from that of national wars, the ideological wars from the wars of mere aggression. But the demarcation is as artificial as such arbitrary divisions commonly are. Aggression, dynastic ambition, and fanaticism are all alike present in the hazy background behind the actual reality of the war, and the last of the wars of religion merged insensibly into the pseudo-national wars of the future.

At Lissa in Poland the Bohemian Protestant exile Comenius wrote: "They have sacrificed us at the treaties of Osnabrück. . . . I conjure you by the wounds of Christ, that you do not forsake us who are persecuted for the sake of Christ." From the Vatican, Innocent X solemnly condemned the peace as "null, void, invalid, iniquitous, unjust, damnable, reprobate, inane, empty of meaning and effect for all time." After thirty years of fighting the extreme Catholics and the extreme Protestants were left still unsatisfied. Both Ferdinand and Christina had to prohibit their clergy from publicly condemning the peace, and the Bull issued with all the prestige of the Vatican was as ineffective in practical politics as the appeal of the exiled Bohemian.

After the expenditure of so much human life to so little purpose, men might have grasped the essential futility of putting the beliefs of the mind to the judgment of the sword. Instead, they rejected religion as an object to fight for and found others.

As there was no compulsion towards a conflict which, in despite of the apparent bitterness of parties, took so long to engage and needed so much assiduous blowing to fan the flame, so no right was vindicated by its ragged end. The war solved no problem. Its effects, both immediate and indirect, were either negative or disastrous. Morally subversive, economically destructive, socially degrading, confused in its causes, devious in its course, futile in its result, it is the outstanding example in European history of meaningless conflict. The overwhelming majority in Europe, the overwhelming majority in Germany, wanted no war; powerless and voiceless, there was no need even to persuade them that they did. The decision was made without thought of them. Yet of those who, one by one, let themselves be drawn into the conflict, few were irresponsible and nearly all were genuinely anxious for an ultimate and better peace. Almost all—one excepts the King of Sweden—were actuated rather by fear than by lust of conquest or passion of faith. They wanted peace and they fought for thirty years to be sure of it. They did not learn then, and have not since, that war breeds only war. . . .

The war has been represented as the cause of almost every German calamity, economic, moral, national and social; it is loosely said to have put German civilization back by two hundred years, whatever that may mean. I do not believe this to be true. On the contrary, I believe the effect of the Thirty Years War on German history to have been greatly and even damagingly exaggerated. The economic decline of Germany ante-dates the war by many years, while Germany's political disintegration was a cause rather than an effect of the war. The after-effects of the war were neither so general, so prolonged nor so disastrous as they have been popularly presented. . . .

[The Thirty Years' War] need not have happened and it settled nothing worth settling. No doubt it assured the replacement of Spain by France as the dominating power in western Europe, an event of some importance in the history of the Western world. But the same result might have been achieved at far less cost and without a generation of war among the Germans who were only very indirectly concerned in the matter at all. Several statesmen of genius outside Germany from time to time dominated the course of the war; no statesman of genius inside Germany appeared to put a stop to it. The dismal course of the conflict, dragging on from one decade to the next and from one deadlock to the next, seems to me an object lesson on the dangers and disasters which can arise when men of narrow hearts and little minds are in high places.

Georges Pagès
THE WAR AS A DIVIDING POINT BETWEEN MEDIEVAL AND MODERN TIMES

Georges Pagès (1867–1939) was born in Paris, and after a career as a school teacher, during which he did research in German archives, he was appointed professor at the University of Paris. He wrote two school books on French history, and a superb study of French administrative history in the sixteenth and seventeenth centuries, The Monarchy of the Old Regime. *His last work, unfinished and completed by V. L. Tapié, was an introduction to early seventeenth century French history,* The Birth of the Great Century. *In the meantime he also established himself as a leading authority on the seventeenth century in general. The fruit of his early researches in Germany was a study of the relations between Brandenburg-Prussia and France in the first half of Louis XIV's reign, and in 1939 he published the book from which the following extracts are taken, the most satisfactory concise narrative of the events of the Thirty Years' War.*

From Georges Pagès, *La Guerre de Trente Ans, 1618–1648,* 2nd ed. (Paris, 1949), pp. 7–8, 16–20, 22–23, 26–28, 33–34 and 263–267. Reprinted by permission of Éditions Payot, Paris. Editor's translation. It has now appeared in an English translation by David Maland and John Hooper (New York, 1970).

I

It is impossible to understand the Thirty Years' War properly if it is studied in isolation. It was only one of the last manifestations of a much larger crisis: the passage from medieval to modern times in all western and central Europe. This crisis was long and slow, its successive changes were not always the same in all countries, and its progress, as far as it can be followed, was full of unexpected twists, stoppages, retreats, and sometimes also abrupt leaps ahead. It was a crisis that lasted for several centuries and cannot be enclosed in a precise chronological framework. Let us say, without giving it too much importance, that it started in the fifteenth century and was hardly over before the middle of the seventeenth. From the point of view of politics, it was marked by the formation of the first modern states; from the point of view of religion, by the destruction of the Christian unity that the Catholic Church achieved in the middle ages, and by the formation of the Protestant churches. However, at the beginning of the seventeenth century this development of a new world, which was already almost complete in western Europe, had hardly started in the central part of the continent. In Germany, where a medieval power, that of the Emperor, survived, and where the fight between Catholicism and Reform was still being fought with the outcome unsure. Here modern Europe managed to establish itself only at the price of thirty years of war. One cannot understand the Germany of that period if one forgets that survivals from the middle ages lasted longer there than anywhere else and also that this country was in the middle of a Europe much further advanced than itself.

Germany cannot even be defined except in relation to what was already a new Europe around it. One can almost say that Germany was precisely that part of Europe where the Middle Ages had not yet given way to modern times. It is impossible to give an ethnic definition of Germany, impossible to include in it all the Germans or to exclude all other races. It is usually confused with the Empire, and this is in fact the only convenient way of approximating its extent, even though there were Germans outside the Empire and non-German inhabitants within the Empire. . . .

At the start of the seventeenth century Germany was a nation not yet unified, even as a nation. The inhabitants spoke different dialects;

they formed distinct groups whose individuality was so vital that it has still not disappeared in the Germany of today. . . . There was a certain national consciousness, a kind of German patriotism. But it manifested itself only in opposition to foreigners. . . .

In this Germany without unity one must note further (and the fact is of prime importance) that there was no correspondence between the natural divisions of the country . . . and its division into political groupings which had been born in feudal times out of the chances of succession or war, and which were called "the principalities and States of the Holy Roman Empire." . . . These were so tangled that it is almost impossible to draw an exact map of Germany in this period. They were infinitely varied in extent, importance and form of government. They had so many different names that one can hardly remember them all: secular principalities and ecclesiastical principalities; among the first were duchies, landgravates, marches (or margravates), counties; among the second were archbishoprics, bishoprics, abbeys; outside the principalities there were urban republics known as free cities; and one must still add the tiny dominions held around a castle, particularly in southern Germany, by the "knights of the Empire."

If this confused mass of "Princes and States" formed any whole, it was only because they composed the Empire, . . . a vast region without fixed limits over which imperial pretensions extended, and where there was not yet a state strong enough to achieve complete independence on its own. . . . [But] in time of danger from abroad they clustered around the Emperor, who was thus the real head of the Empire. . . .

Elected by seven German princes [who had been made electors of the Empire in the fourteenth century], . . . the Emperor, like all the princes, sought to extend his personal possessions and make the best of his rights and pretensions. He also sought to increase his authority as suzerain over the princes of the Empire, and this caused occasional conflicts and a latent antagonism between his pretensions and the ambitions of the princes . . . [which] dominated the internal life of the Empire. But the forms that this antagonism took, the means that it used, depended on the institutions that served to frame the Empire. . . . These did not form a well unified system. They were created one by one to meet the necessities of the day. They succeeded only in making the Empire an informal state, in which many types of states participated but none had any effect. . . .

Who was supposed to keep peace and order among the [many states]? It should have been the Emperor. But he did not always have the means to do so, nor even the desire. . . . It was rare that he had the men necessary to enforce his own decision himself; he was most often reduced to using the troops of some prince of the Empire. . . .

The essential federal institution . . . was the "Diet of the Empire," the *Reichstag*. The Diet represented all the princes and states. . . . There the decisions were taken which concerned the whole Empire and which were to be enforced throughout the Empire. But . . . the Diet was a complicated organism which functioned slowly and with difficulty. It was an assembly where much was said, and even more was written . . . but where little was done. Questions of precedence and juridical arguments . . . took considerable time and prolonged indefinitely deliberations which often never ended. At the beginning of the seventeenth century one could hardly conceal the impotence of the Diet of the Empire. . . .

To understand the Germany of the time properly one must also look at a state, or more precisely a group of states, which was almost entirely a part of the Empire, but which had its own individuality: I mean the states of the House of Austria. The House of Austria, as it was constituted at the beginning of the seventeenth century, was the fairly recent creation of the younger brother of Charles V, Ferdinand of Hapsburg [Ferdinand I]. Already at the time of Charles V Ferdinand reigned with the title of Archduke over Upper and Lower Austria, . . . and over various principalities previously attached to Austria: Styria, Carinthia, Carniola and the Tyrol. In 1526 he had himself elected King of Bohemia by the Bohemian Estates and King of Hungary by the Hungarian Diet. Thus there was formed an artificial group of territories, by different races speaking different languages: German, several Slavic dialects (Czech, Slovak, Slovene, Croatian) and Hungarian. It did not seem that so heterogeneous an assembly could last: it lasted nonetheless, as we know, up to our own days. Ferdinand spent his entire reign consolidating and organizing. . . . At his death, in 1564, his creation was already well established. . . .

The main [consequence of this development worth noting] was the new power the Emperor gained . . . from private possessions of so large an extent. In earlier times Charles V had based his authority as Emperor on enormous territorial power, but his territory was completely distinct from the Empire, and its political center was far from the Empire, in Madrid. The possessions of Ferdinand I and his successors, on the other hand, even those which were peopled primarily by Slavs, were all part of the Empire, with the sole exception of . . . Hungary. And one of the crowns worn by Ferdinand and his successors, that of Bohemia, carried with it the dignity of an Imperial elector. It was no small matter that the Emperor was at the same time head of the most powerful princely house in the Empire. . . . Nor was it a small matter that the Emperor was the brother (in Ferdinand I's time), then the uncle, and then the cousin of the King of Spain; that the same family, the Hapsburgs, if not the same sovereign, ruled in Vienna and Madrid, and that the Austrian branch of the House of Hapsburg could very often count, in times of peril, on the Spanish branch.

But on the other hand the position of the House of Austria could have grave consequences for the destiny of Germany. The interests of the House of Austria and the interests of Germany were not always the same. The Emperor, head of the House of Austria, necessarily had to have two policies: an Imperial, that is to say a German, policy, and a peculiarly Austrian policy. It occasionally happened that his Austrian policy made him misunderstand the interests of Germany. Furthermore, the Emperor's German and Austrian policies were complicated from time to time, and increasingly so, by a dynastic policy that one can call purely "Hapsburgian." When this began, the great crisis which forms the subject of this study developed, and we will see how relations between Vienna and Madrid, how the influence of Spanish policy on Imperial policy, aggravated this crisis and forced the states neighboring the Empire to intervene in some way, which in turn transformed it into a European crisis. . . .

[As for religion,] it is difficult to indicate precisely how the Catholics and Protestants divided the Empire at the beginning of the seventeenth century. One must not forget that the Counter Reformation had not achieved its last success. The positions were not as yet stabilized. . . .

The Peace of Augsburg, far from ending the religious and political troubles that emerged from the Reformation, marked the beginning of a long period of cold war in the Empire, during which the violent crisis which we call the Thirty Years' War was prepared. Above all, two circumstances connected with the peace made the crisis inevitable.

The first was a direct consequence of the manner in which the peace was concluded. The Diet which negotiated it remained its sole guarantee. In case of litigations (and . . . they were frequent), it was to the Diet that Protestants or Catholics had to address themselves. But here, as elsewhere, the Diet revealed its impotence. It soon became only too evident that the institutions of the Empire could not assure the princes, and the Protestant princes in particular, the protection they had the right to expect. So there began a kind of dissolution of the Empire which the war, a little later, hastened. . . .

The second circumstance was the increasing growth of the reformed faith. It continued to spread into the Rhineland, southern Germany, Upper and Lower Austria, and Hungary. On the very next day after the peace an Elector, the Palatine prince Frederick III, openly declared himself a Calvinist. Others followed. . . . But the Calvinists were not included in the peace. . . . They were thus a foreign body within the Empire, outside the protection of the laws of the Empire. . . . The Calvinist princes were forced to defend themselves on their own, either by uniting or by seeking alliances with foreign princes. They were to be the first to take up arms against the Emperor.

Moreover, they were not the only ones acting outside the framework of the peace. Many Catholics were doing the same. Their activities were conducted by the great religious orders, the Capuchins and the Jesuits. They were concerned less with respecting the terms of the peace than with recapturing souls that had been led away from the Roman Church by the Reformation. . . . The Capuchins preached everywhere. The Society of Jesus founded colleges everywhere which produced the defenders of the Faith: the first two, one at Prague and the other at Ingolstadt in Bavaria, where Maximilian of Bavaria and Ferdinand II were raised, were founded in 1556. Catholicism resumed the offensive. And almost at the same time—in 1563—the decrees of the Council of Trent established dogma and condemned all Protestant innovations. A little later the Jesuit Bellarmine commented on the decrees of the Council in resounding works which were widely circulated in Germany and inspired almost all the German episcopacy.

It was therefore not surprising that, in a Germany so torn apart by the greed of princes and the passions of religion, a local revolt, but one which seemed to imperil the very existence of the House of Austria, should have been sufficient to involve at first almost all Germany, and then even the neighbors of the Empire, in a war that was one of the most frightful of modern times. . . .

II

Too many historians have insisted on the depopulation and distress of Germany at the end of the Thirty Years' War for it to be profitable to do so again. The extent of the ravages caused by the war explains the way contemporaries almost always qualified the peace that brought it to a close as the peace "so dearly bought." They held on to this peace determinedly; it endured; the villages were rebuilt, the population increased again, trade reappeared along abandoned routes, prosperity returned. All the same, some of the social transformations that took place during the war and were among its consequences remained. I am thinking in particular of the deterioration of the lot of the peasant classes, their enserfment by landowners. The beneficiaries of the peace were above all the territorial princes and nobility, though it is true that when the atrocities committed by the soldiery stopped, the rural population gained from the peace a little more security in the midst of misery.

One would be wrong to believe that a new Germany was born out of the peace. If religious passions no longer played the same role as before in the Empire, that was because they had already worked themselves out during the war. As for the political transformations, their origins lay far in the past. The Peace of Westphalia confirmed them and gave them the guarantee of a contractual right: it did not create them. . . . The result of the weakening of the Emperor's power in the Empire was that the Emperor took less interest in the internal life of Germany and occupied himself more with his personal states. . . . Austria devoted itself more and more to its eastern mission.

Germany did not escape the contagion of ideas of royal absolutism which had already swept through all western Europe. Yet the reinforcement of sovereign power was not carried out for the benefit of the Emperor in the framework of the Empire; but instead for the benefit of certain princes in the narrower framework of certain states of the Empire: states such as Bavaria and that other state whose vitality was revealed during the last years of the war, . . . the state of the Hohenzollerns [Brandenburg-Prussia]. . . . It was in this strengthening of the best situated or best governed principalities that the future of Germany, from the eighteenth century on, was prepared. The way was opened, too, for the birth, still uncertain, of a kind of German nationalism. The impotence of the disunited princes during the war gave birth, among a few of them, to a desire for unity. . . .

As opposed to this Germany which still sought its destiny, France and Sweden appeared to be the victorious powers in 1648. Sweden had achieved a position in northern Europe which, as has often been said, did not correspond to its true strength. A small country, poor in men and natural resources, . . . it had become in a few years a great military power, thanks to the genius and audacity of Gustavus Adolphus. It considered itself mistress of the Baltic. It is easy for us to say, with the hindsight of history, that Sweden could not have sustained for long a role for which it was not destined by nature. Contemporaries thought otherwise. . . . Sweden's decline was not yet apparent. Louis XIV . . . was to continue to seek a Swedish alliance. . . . It is true that France, with its population larger than any other country in Europe, with its abundance of resources of all kinds, seemed destined to reap a greater profit than Sweden from the disarray of Germany after the peace. But we must take into account that in 1648 France's internal situation forebode a grave crisis whose outcome could not be foreseen. The King of Spain did not yet consider himself defeated, and hoped to gain his revenge. . . . [Only] the peace with Spain ten to twelve years later was to make the results of the German peace definitive.

The contemporaries of the Peace of Westphalia realized only slowly, and much later, that around the middle of the seventeenth century a new period began in European history. . . .

With the Thirty Years' War there came to an end the crisis which brought modern out of medieval Europe. The Thirty Years' War witnessed the last effort of the Roman Church and the House of Hapsburg to reestablish unity by a victory of Catholicism over Protestant heresies and the renewal of the universal power of the Emperor. If the Church and the House of Austria had succeeded, perhaps the ideal of the Middle Ages, the "Christian republic," governed in common by Emperor and Pope, would have been restored. But they could not have succeeded, because the evolution of new political and religious concepts had already advanced too far. They failed. Instead of the unity of the Christian world, the Peace of Westphalia substituted—without saying so openly—the idea of a system of independent states, a kind of international society. It was a society which concerned itself neither with the type of government within its component states—monarchies, principalities, or republics—nor with the religious confessions which prevailed in them. Europe thus became a secular system (at the international level) of independent states. We are at the dawn of the principle of nationalities.

This profound transformation of Europe, which was achieved during the last convulsions of the Thirty Years' War, this definitive break with the past, was undoubtedly powerfully helped by France, and particularly by Cardinal Richelieu. . . . He realized that only a league of Protestant powers, sustained and led by his king, could prevent the House of Hapsburg from establishing its hegemony over Europe. He hoped . . . to maintain an equilibrium between the two parties and to save for Catholicism at least that position which it had preserved or reconquered. He succeeded. It is no less certain that, in order to succeed, he accepted a kind of secularization of European politics, as well as the division of Europe into distinct churches and states, that is to say a new international law, all of whose consequences are not yet exhausted. It was thus French policy—the policy of Richelieu—that, by enlarging the Thirty Years' War, created modern Europe as it already appeared, in its essential characteristics, at the Peace of Westphalia.

S. H. Steinberg

THE NOT SO DESTRUCTIVE, NOT SO RELIGIOUS, AND NOT PRIMARILY GERMAN WAR

S. H. Steinberg was born in Germany in 1899. He studied at Munich and Leipzig and then taught at the University of Leipzig. After moving to England, he did research at the Courtauld Institute in London and taught for a while at an English school. He has been an editor of Chamber's Encyclopaedia *and* Cassell's Encyclopaedia of Literature. *His first book was a short survey history of Germany, published in 1944. Since that time he has produced an excellent history of printing which has gone through many editions in a number of languages; a book of historical tables; and a dictionary of English history. The article from which the following selections are taken was the first comprehensive attempt to bring together all the major criticisms that had been levelled at the traditional view of the Thirty Years' War. It appeared in 1947.*

The author of the most recent book on the "Thirty Years' War" sums up its causes and results as follows.

> The larger issue was that between the dynasties of Hapsburg and Bourbon. . . . But . . . the geography and politics of Germany alone give the key to the problem. The signal for war was given . . . in May 1618, by revolt in Bohemia. There was no compulsion towards a conflict. . . . The war solved no problem. Its effects, both immediate and indirect, were either negative or disastrous. Morally subversive, economically destructive, socially degrading, confused in its causes, devious in its course, futile in its result, it is the outstanding example in European history of meaningless conflict.

Apart from the first dozen words quoted here almost every word of this statement is debatable. However, Miss Wedgwood only voices what may be called the *consensus gentium;* and it will take time and patience to uproot the prejudices and misconceptions of historians which have been strongly backed by playwrights, novelists and poets. To Miss Wedgwood's version the following may be opposed. The various European wars fought between 1609 and 1660 decided the

From S. H. Steinberg, "The Thirty Years' War: A New Interpretation," *History* 32 (September 1947): 89–102. Reprinted by permission of the author and the Historical Association, London.

issue between the dynasties of Hapsburg and Bourbon. France's need to break her encirclement gives the key to the problem. Open warfare ensued over the Hapsburg effort to strengthen their grip on France to the north and northeast (truce with the Netherlands and attempted seizure of Jülich-Cleves, April 1609). The only alternative to armed conflict was tame submission to Hapsburg domination. The series of wars ending with the Peace of the Pyrenees (1659) solved the outstanding problem of Europe: the final overthrow of Hapsburg hegemony established the principle of the balance of power, which henceforth would militate against every attempt to set up a single-state rule over Europe. The immediate effects of most of the wars were negligible; cumulatively and indirectly, they were momentous. Morally, the age of rationalism affirmed the equality of the Christian denominations and, implicitly, the freedom of worship and thought; economically, the age of mercantilism rid Europe from the curse of the American gold which had wrecked the economics of the sixteenth century; socially, the age of absolutism dissolved the feudal structure of society. It is the outstanding example in European history of an intrinsically successful settlement.

The traditional concept of the Thirty Years' War is based on two main groups of sources: deliberate official propaganda and unwittingly one-sided private records. The first reflect the opinions of the victorious powers—France, Sweden, the Netherlands, Brandenburg; the second, those of the educated middle class which was hit hardest by the economic upheaval of the time. That these distortions should have gained credence may perhaps be ascribed to two failings of the nineteenth-century schools of German historians: they consciously or unconsciously made the political interests of the Prussian monarchy the criterion by which they judged the course of German history; and they preferred narrative sources and dispositive documents to administrative and business records.

Now of the two German powers which gained most by the Peace of Westphalia—Brandenburg and Bavaria—the latter lapsed into a state of indolence and complacency after the death of Maximilian I (1651), whereas in the former, Frederick William I, the Great Elector, pursued a vigorous policy of aggrandizement. He was a master of political propaganda, the first to put over the identification of Hohenzollern and German interests; and he laid the foundations of the Prussian monarchy in the ideological sphere as well as in that of power politics. In Samuel von Pufendorf (1632–1694) he secured as court historiographer a scholar and pamphleteer of European reputation who had already served the Dutch, Swedish and Palatine governments. Pufendorf's interpretation of the Thirty Years' War was taken up by Frederick the Great in his *Mémoires pour servir à l'histoire de la maison de Brandebourg,* and has become part and parcel of the national-liberal historiography of the nineteenth century.

The original "atrocity" propaganda emanating from Berlin had a double aim: for home consumption it was meant to accentuate the magnitude of the political, economic and cultural successes, real or alleged, of the Great Elector by painting the background as black as possible; while at the same time the darker aspects of his policy—the abandonment of the peasantry to the tender mercies of the Junkers, the oppressive taxation of the poorer classes in general and of the townspeople in particular, the tax exemption of the Junkers, and the inordinate expenses for the standing army—could, to the more gullible, be justified as unavoidable consequences of the war. As an Instrument of foreign policy, the Brandenburg version of the Thirty Years' War—Brandenburg as the defender of the Protestant religion and of the "German liberties" against Hapsburg interference and foreign aggression in general—was meant to serve the shifts and vagaries of the Great Elector's policy: one aspect or another of this picture could always be turned against his *pro tempore* enemy—the emperor, Sweden, Poland, France, Denmark—and incidentally win for him the moral support of the German and Dutch Protestants or of the anti-Hapsburg German Catholic princes, or the latent German patriotism of the liberal professions.

This picture of the Thirty Years' War, born of the needs of the Brandenburg propaganda of 1650–1690, more or less coincided with the historical preconceptions of nineteenth-century national liberalism. The current version of the Thirty Years' War therefore largely reflects the Prusso-German attitude of Bismarck's fight against the German middle states, Austria and France, the *Kulturkampf* against the Roman Church, and the cultural and economic expansionism of the Hohenzollern Empire.

While the official records reflect the light in which the victorious party wished the nexus and causality of events to be seen, the private sources—chronicles, annals, diaries, letters—chiefly show the results of the war as experienced by those who lost most. These documents have been used to fill in the lurid details of famine and starvation, epidemics and cannibalism, ruin of town and country, decline of civilization, extinction of large sections of the population and complete pauperization of the remainder. It is not the purpose of the present paper to glorify the Thirty Years' War; and much misery, brutality, cruelty and suffering no doubt added to the terror and slaughter of purely military actions. But nothing is gained by putting the Thirty Year's War in a class by itself: its destructive aspects are common to every war—and were in any case smaller than those of "total war" in the twentieth century—and an impartial assessment of the facts will lead to the conclusion that some of the features most commonly attributed to it are unconnected with the war itself, while others have been generalized and exaggerated. The generalization of isolated events, the exaggeration of facts and, above all, figures, the special pleading for a particular cause, lay the contemporary chroniclers and diarists less open to criticism than modern historians who have failed to recognize the distorted perspective from which these accounts have been written: for the compilers of town chronicles, parish registers, family albums and personal diaries, all belonged to the same class of educated, professional men—clerks, priests, officials, lawyers —who were hit by every vicissitude of the times, and always hit hardest. Whenever circumstances forced upon the treasury a cut in expenditure, it was the educational and cultural departments which were the first victims.

The very term "Thirty Years' War" is fraught with misunderstanding. Seventeenth-century authors speak of the military events of the first half of the century as "wars," *"bella"* in the plural and clearly distinguish between the *"bellum Bohemicum," "bellum Suecicum"* and so forth. The figure "thirty" and the singular "war" seems to occur for the first time in Pufendorf's *De statu imperii Germanici* (1667). One of the liveliest and still most readable pamphlets of seventeenth-century political science, its success was immediate and far-reaching: German, French, English and Dutch translations, popular adaptations and polemical treatises secured the rapid spread of its arguments throughout Europe. Here we have already all the well-known theses of later historians: the Bohemian revolt of 1618 as the

FIGURE 2. *The Beast of War.* During the seventeenth century, before the age of newspapers, the chief means of communication and propaganda was the broadside. A single sheet of paper, easily produced and sold, it usually featured a scurrilous cartoon and verse that ridiculed leaders of the war or the opposition. This example, however, is different—an antiwar broadside describing the "beast" of war. As the title puts it, this "gruesome beast . . . has destroyed the larger part of Germany in just a few years." (*Courtesy of Stadtbibliothek of Ulm*)

beginning, the Peace of Westphalia as the end of the war; its character as a religious conflict; its extension over the whole of Germany; the omission of its European setting; the economic ruin and exhaustion; and the insinuation that Austria is a foreign power like France and Turkey.

From the political point of view the Thirty Years' War offers two aspects: the general European, and the particular German one. Both issues can be traced to the foreign and home policies of the emperors Maximilian I and Charles V. In the European field, Maximilian started the antagonism between the houses of Hapsburg and Valois by claiming the inheritance of Charles the Bold of Burgundy, and made it permanent by marrying his only son to the daughter and heiress of the Spanish world-monarchy. He thereby welded a ring of Hapsburg possessions round France which every French statesman was bound to try his utmost to break.

In Germany, Maximilian deliberately wrecked the last prospect of equitable settlement of the constitutional dispute between centralism and federalism. As at the same time the imperial crown became hereditary in the house of Hapsburg, in all but legal prescription, he made this dynasty the permanent champion of that centralism which had become unattainable and was therefore by force of circumstances reactionary; so that any combination of forces, which for different reasons might be opposed to the Hapsburgs or the empire or centralization, might appear as fighting for progress.

Charles V, Maximilian's grandson, intensified this development. He completed the total encirclement of France by acquiring the duchy of Milan, subduing the papacy, and drawing Portugal, England, Denmark and Poland into the Hapsburg orbit. The very greatness of his successes made a reaction inevitable. The exploits of Elizabethan England, the secession of the Spanish Netherlands, the alliance between France and the German Protestants (1552), the pacification of France by the edict of Nantes (1598)—are all signs of the growing restiveness against Hapsburg universalism. In fact, during the fifty years following the death of Charles V (1558) all European powers were jockeying for position.

France was obviously the rallying point of every opponent of Hapsburg domination throughout the whole of western Europe and the New World. The aggressive and expansionist policies of Louis XIV and Napoleon I have obliterated the fact that up to the death of Mazarin (1661) it was France which was the protagonist of the European balance of power against the domination of the continent by a single power.

The political struggle was accompanied by an ideological struggle. The antagonism between the old and the new faith made itself felt in the early stages of the conflict, and religious catchwords and propaganda were meant as sincerely or insincerely as were in more recent times the slogans of democracy and totalitarianism. The Hapsburgs, it is true, represented all the life-forces and the spirit of the reformed church of Rome; and the defeat of the Hapsburgs undoubtedly benefited the Protestant powers of Sweden, the Netherlands, England and Brandenburg. But the victory was chiefly a victory of Catholic France, which during the war was successively led by two cardinals of the Roman church; and the papacy itself had from 1523 to 1644 consistently opposed the Hapsburgs and even lent its support to the Protestant hero, Gustavus Adolphus of Sweden.

France could become the ideological leader of Europe as well as its political protagonist as she herself had solved the fight between Protestantism and Catholicism in a *tertium quid* which transcended both these sixteenth-century points of argument. Because the French leaders—the Protestants Henry IV and Sully and the Catholics Richelieu and Mazarin alike—recognized that the absolute claims inherent in every religious system were irreconcilable, they replaced religious standards by the criterion of the *raison d'état*. This enabled France to destroy Protestantism within her own frontiers and to save Protestantism in Germany, Sweden and the Low Countries, to secure religious unity at home, and to perpetuate the split of western Christendom abroad. Catholic apologists tried in vain to counter this onslaught of secularism by elaborating a *ragione della chiesa;* it has never been a serious challenge to the *raison d'état*.

Seen against this European background, German affairs are of minor importance. Germany, as such, that is the "German section of the Holy Roman Empire," was not at all involved in any of the European wars of the period. The individual German states entered and left one war or another as partisans of the European antagonists; only the emperor was engaged in every conflict, not, however, as German king, but as the head of the Austrian branch of the house of Hapsburg. The German wars started in 1609 with the war of the Jülich-Cleves succession and ended in 1648 with the treaties of Münster and Osnabrück. They decided the political future of the empire, in that the last attempt to set up a centralistic government was defeated in favor of a loose confederation of virtually independent states. The concerted action by which the electors forced the emperor to dismiss his generalissimo Wallenstein in 1630 was their last achievement as a corporate body. They, too, who for centuries had represented the federal principle of the German constitution, henceforth showed an ever diminishing concern with the affairs of the empire and were content to look after their own interests. However, the constitution agreed upon in 1648 proved its soundness in that it lasted for more than 200 years, until 1866, with the short interval of the Napoleonic settlement. The wars also decided the dynastic rivalries within the leading German houses—curiously, every time in favor of the younger branch: the Palatine Wittelsbachs, the Thuringian Wettiners and the Wolfen-büttel Guelphs had to give way to their cousins of Bavaria, Saxony and Hanover, who henceforth formed the leading group of German powers. The most far-reaching result, however, was the rise of the electorate of Brandenburg, before 1609 the least important of the bigger principalities; it came to equal Bavaria and Saxony and was to outstrip them in the following century.

The conception of the Thirty Years' War as a "war of religion" has been abandoned to a large extent since it has been recognized that religious divisions coincided largely with political, constitutional and economic ones. It will always remain a matter of dispute which of these motives was decisive at a given moment. It does, however, seem that rational considerations of political and economic gains determined the policies of the cabinets to the same extent to which religious emotions held a strong sway over the masses, sufficient to whip up their passions in battle and to make them endure with fortitude their plight in adversity. The Swedes, under Gustavus, fought for the pure gospel, caring little for the *"dominium maris Baltici"* and knowing nothing of the French subsidies on which they subsisted; while Tilly's men were fired by an equal zeal for the Holy Virgin, with no stake in the power politics of the Wittelsbachs and ignorant of the pope's support of the heretic Swede.

Political and dynastic, religious and personal motives are inextricably mixed in the actions of the champions of the Protestant and Catholic causes. Both Gustavus Adolphus of Sweden and Maximilian of Bavaria were fervent devotees of their creeds. At the same time, the Lutheran establishment was also Gustavus's strongest bulwark against the claims to the Swedish throne, made by his Catholic cousin, Sigismund of Poland; and as the Palatine Wittelsbachs had assumed the leadership of the Protestant estates of the empire, the head of the Bavarian branch found safety and prospect of gain in rallying the Catholic princes under his standard. The struggle for the *"dominium maris Baltici"* set Gustavus in opposition to Protestant Denmark, Catholic Poland and Orthodox Russia. The occupation of the Hartz mines by the imperial forces (1624) endangered the Swedish copper market; Wallenstein's appointment as "General of the Atlantic and Baltic Seas" (1628) threatened Sweden's maritime position: her vital interests demanded armed intervention against the Catholic Hapsburgs and alliance with Catholic France, and the edict of the restitution (1629) only added religious zeal to the dictates of power politics. Likewise, political considerations brought Maximilian into conflict with the Lutheran imperial cities of Swabia and Franconia, Catholic Austria and Spain, and the Calvinistic Netherlands and Palatinate; but after he had overawed the cities and, in alliance with Austria and Spain, crushed the elector Palatine, his interests as a prince of the empire and member of the college of electors made him turn against the Hapsburgs as his chief opponents. The reduction of the dominant position of the emperor and the removal of the Spaniards from the empire were from 1627 onward his overriding aims which, in cooperation with the pope, Catholic France and Lutheran Saxony, were brought to a successful consummation.

The ruinous effect of the war years on German economic and cultural life has been very much exaggerated. War is by its very nature destructive, and the wars of the seventeenth century are no exceptions. But all the campaigns of the period 1609–1648 were of short duration and the armies themselves of a very small size. It was only the districts of primary strategic importance which had to bear the brunt of successive invasions in the seventeenth century, as they have been the focal points of every fight in central Europe, from Caesar's to Eisenhower's campaigns: the Rhine crossings of Breisach and Wesel, the Leipzig plain, the passes across the Black Forest and the roads to Regensburg and the Danube Valley. Other tracts of Germany were hardly affected at all, some only for a few weeks; the majority of towns never saw an enemy inside their walls.

From the middle of the thirteenth century the towns were the undisputed masters of German economics. Even agriculture, if not brought under direct control of city financiers, was at least completely dependent upon the town markets for home consumption as well as exportation (with the notable exception of the Teutonic Order in Prussia, whose totalitarian economy comprised production as well as commerce and excluded the citizen middlemen). This whole system of German economics was breaking down in a series of disastrous events from the middle of the sixteenth century: the south German cities were ruined by the repeated bankruptcies of the Spanish crown (1557, 1575, 1596, 1607), in which they lost every financial gain accumulated in the preceding century. The Hanse towns of North Germany were equally hit by the sack of Antwerp (1576) and the closing of the London Steelyard (1598) which deprived them of the two western pillars of their trading system; and even more by the separation of the Netherlands from Spain. The new republic vigorously asserted its independence in the economic sphere, intruding into the Baltic trade, hitherto the jealously-guarded monopoly of the Hanse.

About 1620 the German towns still presented an outward picture of opulence and solidity—very much emphasized to the casual observer by the splendor of their architectural achievements. . . . Yet the foundations of their prosperity had gone, and the big inflation of the years 1619–1623 only set the seal upon the utter ruin of German economics which had started some fifty years earlier.

In reality, the crisis of the inflation was the fever which preceded the patient's recovery. The contemporaries of the "clippers and counterfeiters of coins" (*Kipper und Wipper*) were altogether nonplussed by the upheaval of all standards of financial honesty and security, especially as the devaluation of currency was worst in the countries whose prolific output of silver had made them appear the very pillars of affluence and stability: the petty principality of Brunswick-Wolfenbüttel had thirty-two mints operating in 1622, and the emperor Ferdinand II lent his active support to a combine of racketeers who exploited Austria, Bohemia and Moravia for three or four years. When by 1624 the currency was stabilized again, a violent and thorough-going transfer of property had occurred; hardly any of the old firms of international repute survived, and successful speculators, army con-tractors and black marketeers took their place, many of them Jews and newly converted Roman Catholics, of whom Wallenstein was to become the most conspicuous. All through the following decades, this change-over of family and business fortunes continued: the proscrip-tion of Wallenstein and his lieutenants in 1634 threw the biggest and best estates of Bohemia and Silesia upon the market; the new princi-ples of the "mercantilist" system of economics gave openings to fresh and quick brains, and the losses sustained by the one were counter-balanced by the gains of the other. On the whole, the national in-come, productive power and standard of living were higher about 1650 than they had been fifty years earlier.

The part of the economic structure which was hit hardest by the immediate effects of the war was agriculture, especially for medium sized and small farmers. To big landowners, on the other hand, the war itself, the maintenance of troops over wide distances and the new methods of logistics and commissariat as introduced by Wallenstein and Gustavus Adolphus, offered fresh possibilities of enrichment. In fact, the seventeenth century is the period of the growth of the big *latifundia* of the Junkers at the smallholders' expense. The eviction of peasants, and the sequestration of peasant land by the lord of the manor had started at the end of the sixteenth century, caused by the steady rise of corn prices which made large-scale farming and bulk selling more profitable. The depopulation of the countryside and the disappearance of whole villages were in full swing before the first shot of the Thirty Years' War was fired, and went on long after the conclusion of the Peace of Westphalia.

On the other hand, the improved organization of the commissariat resulted in increasing the apparent burdens of occupied countries. Indiscriminate pillaging by a band of marauders may have done greater damage, but it appeared as a natural phenomenon, whereas the methodical requisitioning by quartermasters was felt the more irksome as it was planned and therefore rigid, thorough and therefore inescapable, fixed in writing and therefore long remembered and resented.

Ignorance of scientific demography and inability to visualize large figures account for the legend of the enormous loss of population, which is variously given as ranging from a third to half or more of the total. All these figures are purely imaginary. Such statistical surveys as were occasionally made were always designed to support some special pleading: to obtain a grant in aid, a reduction of payments, or an alleviation of services. The main sources, however, are contemporary reports and, rarely, records of deaths, to the virtual exclusion of registers of births. In view of the huge birthrate this neglect amounts to 30 to 50 percent; in other words, exactly that third or half by which the population is said to have been reduced. It is, of course, indisputable that the irregular movements of troops, especially of ill-disciplined mercenaries, and the migration of refugees greatly contributed to the spreading of epidemics, such as the various kinds of typhoid (the greatest terror of the seventeenth century) or, to a lesser degree, of the plague and syphilis. On the other hand, the mortality of the urban population shows a surprising likeness in a place which was far remote from the European battlefields, and one which was right in their midst: it has been computed at seventy *per mille* for London in 1620–1643, and at sixty-eight *per mille* for Frankfurt in 1600–1650.

What actually happened was an extensive inner migration chiefly from the agrarian countryside into the industrial town, and from the economically retrograde town to the prosperous one. As with the ownership of movable and immovable property, so with regard to the population it is more appropriate to speak of redistribution than of destruction.

The net result is that of an all-round, though very limited increase. This almost imperceptible rise, and over long periods, virtual stagnation, is characteristic of every community of a predominantly agricultural type. Keeping in mind the vagueness of the term "Germany," it seems safe to assume a population of fifteen to seventeen million in 1600. A loss of five to eight million by 1650 could not possibly have been made good by 1700, for which year a population of seventeen to twenty million is fairly well documented.

The legend of cultural exhaustion and desolation as a concomitant and result of the Thirty Years' War is perhaps easiest to refute. It is solely due to the aesthetic standards of nineteenth-century criticism in literature, art, architecture and music. The culture of the seventeenth century is essentially baroque; and "baroque" was anathema to the critics of the nineteenth century, as "gothic" had been to those of the eighteenth. The revaluation which has taken place within the last thirty years or so makes unnecessary a defense of the writers, architects and musicians of the period of the Thirty Years' War. The war itself had little, and certainly no detrimental influence upon the cultural life of Germany. . . .

The Thirty Years' War, put in its proper perspective, was therefore not such a catastrophe as popular historians have made out. Perhaps the one irreparable damage Germany sustained in the first half of the seventeenth century was that German civilization and German politics parted company. This separation may be the greatest misfortune of German history.

Carl J. Friedrich
THE RELIGIOUS MOTIVE REAFFIRMED

Carl J. Friedrich is a professor both in the government department at Harvard University and at Heidelberg University in Germany. Born in Germany in 1901, he studied at Heidelberg before eventually coming to the United States. He is a distinguished authority on political thought, constitutional law and constitutional history, and he has written widely on these subjects. He has long been interested in the seventeenth century, which is the subject of his book The Age of Power *as well as the book from which the following selections are taken,* The Age of the Baroque.

I

It has been the fashion to minimize the religious aspect of the great wars which raged in the heart of Europe, over the territory of the Holy Roman Empire of the German Nation. Not only the calculating statecraft of Richelieu and Mazarin, but even Pope Urban VIII's own insistence lent support to such a view in a later age which had come to look upon religion and politics as fairly well separated fields of thought and action. Liberal historians found it difficult to perceive that for baroque man religion and politics were cut from the same cloth, indeed that the most intensely political issues were precisely the religious ones. Gone was the neopaganism of the Renaissance, with its preoccupation with self-fulfillment here and now. Once again, and for the last time, life was seen as meaningful in religious, even theological terms, and the greater insight into power which the Renaissance had brought served merely to deepen the political passion brought to the struggle over religious faiths.

Without a full appreciation of the close links between secular and religious issues, it becomes impossible to comprehend the Thirty Years' War. Frederick, the unlucky Palatine, as well as Ferdinand, Tilly and Gustavus Adolphus, Maximilian of Bavaria and John George of Saxony—they all must be considered fools unless their religious motivation is understood as the quintessential core of their politics. Time and again, they appear to have done the "wrong thing," if their actions are viewed in a strictly secular perspective. To be sure, men became increasingly sophisticated as the war dragged on; but even after peace was finally concluded in 1648, the religious controversies continued. Ever since the Diet of Augsburg (1555) had adopted the callous position that a man must confess the religion of those who had authority over the territory he lived in—a view which came to be known under the slogan of *"cujus regio, ejus religio"*—the intimate tie of religion and government had been the basis of the Holy Empire's tenuous peace. Born of the spirit of its time—Lutheran otherworldliness combining with Humanistic indifferentism—this doctrine was no more than an unstable compromise between Catholics and Lutherans, the Calvinists being entirely outside its protective sphere. But in the seventeenth century not only the Calvinists, who by 1618 had become the fighting protagonists of Protestantism, but likewise the more ardent Catholics, inspired by the Council of Trent, by the Jesuits and Capuchins, backed by the power of Spain and filled with the ardor of the Counter Reformation, had come to look upon this doctrine as wicked and contrary to their deepest convictions.

When Ferdinand, after claiming the crown of Bohemia by heredity, proceeded to push the work of counter reformation, his strongest motivation was religious; so was the resistance offered by the

Bohemian people, as well as Frederick's acceptance of the crown of Bohemia on the basis of an election. Dynastic and national sentiments played their part, surely, but they reinforced the basic religious urge. The same concurrence of religious with dynastic, political, even economic motives persisted throughout the protracted struggle, but the religious did not cease to be the all-pervasive feeling; baroque man, far from being bothered by the contradictions, experienced these polarities as inescapable.

If religion played a vital role in persuading Ferdinand II to dismiss his victorious general [because Wallenstein was reluctant to enforce the Edict of Restitution], it was even more decisive in inspiring Gustavus Adolphus to enter the war against both the emperor and the League. The nineteenth century, incapable of feeling the religious passions which stirred baroque humanity and much impressed with the solidified national states which the seventeenth century bequeathed to posterity, was prone to magnify the dynastic and often Machiavellian policies adopted by rulers who professed to be deeply religious, and the twentieth century has largely followed suit in denying the religious character of these wars. But it is precisely this capacity to regard the statesman as the champion of religion, to live and act the drama of man's dual dependence upon faith and power that constituted the quintessence of the baroque. The Jesuits, sponsors of the baroque style in architecture all over central and southern Europe, advised Catholic rulers, but more especially Ferdinand II, concerning their dual duties. The somber and passionate driving force behind so much unscrupulousness was religious pathos in all its depth. What the Catholics did, elicited a corresponding pattern of thought and action in the Protestant world: Maurice of Nassau and James I, Gustavus Adolphus and Cromwell, as well as many minor figures of the European theater, conceived of themselves as guardians of the "secrets of rule," the *arcana imperii,* to be employed for the greater glory of God and the Christian religion. . . .

II

In spite of the tendency of historical scholarship to tone down the doleful tales which are traditionally associated with the Thirty Years' War, there can be little doubt that its effects were not only disastrous in terms of the immediate future, but that the aftereffects of this war thwarted German life for a hundred years. It was only in the period of Goethe and Schiller that the German people seemed to shake off the pallor that had hung over the nation's cultural life. To be sure, there were noble exceptions, such as Leibniz and Bach, but on the whole the loss in human creative talent as well as the material devastation in town and country could not be overcome until after a long convalescence. Even worse, in the long run, was the institutional confusion which the war brought about. The perpetuation of a vast array of principalities large and small could only serve to prevent the growth of a healthy national spirit related to a suitable government and constitution. For a system of social order and government which had served well enough within the context of the medieval unity of church and empire could in the age of the sovereign state and nation lead only to endless frustrations and eventual violence in the search for a solution. It may be a bit farfetched to trace an explanation of the violence of Fascist nationalism in Germany back to the Thirty Years' War.[1] But that the "monstrosity" which the young Pufendorf saw in the German constitution had something to do with the rise of Prussia few will deny. In any case, the Thirty Years' War marked the effective end of the medieval dream of universal empire, until the revolutionary first Napoleon revived it on a novel basis. . . .

All in all, the toll in human suffering resulting from this greatest of the religious wars was staggering, the results in terms of the religious objectives practically nil. The high hopes of Ferdinand II and his Counter Reformation associates were finished, as were the Calvinists' projects for a predominantly Protestant Empire. The activities on both sides had merely succeeded in demonstrating that rather than surrendering their religious convictions, Germans would divide permanently into many principalities, each governed according to the formula of the religious peace of Augsburg: *"Cujus regio, ejus religio."* A vicious doctrine on the face of it, it nonetheless provided a tolerable compromise for the Germans as a people; a man could remove from one "sovereignty" to another, if compelled by religious scruples. Thus religion triumphed, in a negative sense, over the political requirements of building a modern national state. The outcome

[1] This aspect is suggested in Peter Viereck's imaginative, if somewhat exaggerated, *Metapolitics: From the Romantics to Hitler* (1941).

of the Thirty Years' War in this sense permanently shaped the course of German history, in contrast with England and France, where the religious wars led, eventually, to a consolidation of religious views, favoring Protestant predominance in one, Catholic in the other. To modify the "forcing of conscience" inherent in such unity, religious toleration—the willingness to let the individual decide for himself—served as the pathmaker for a later more pronounced individualism. In Germany, each "state" patriarchially protected the individual's conscience, while the nation remained a cultural community without firm political framework. Protestant Prussia and Saxony, Catholic Austria and Bavaria, not to mention the dozens of lesser princes, nobles and "free" cities, could proceed to develop a political absolutism, untempered by cultural aspirations. The fatal split in German thought and action between the realm of the spirit and the realm of material power had been started. The modern state emerged from the Treaty of Westphalia in all the kingdoms, duchies and principalities, but it was a crippled, barebones "state," a mere apparatus—a bureaucracy serving princely aspirations for power and aggrandizement. The nation remained outside.

J. V. Polišenský

SOCIAL AND ECONOMIC CHANGE AND THE EUROPEAN-WIDE WAR

Josef V. Polišenský, born in 1915, has studied at Prague, Geneva, London, and Oxford. Since receiving his Ph.D. in 1945 he has taught at various universities in Czechoslovakia, England, and Germany, and since 1951 he has been professor of history at the University of Prague. He has published numerous studies of Czech history, dealing mainly with the seventeenth century, and with the Thirty Years' War in particular. An important study of English policy during the Bohemian revolt appeared in 1949, another on Dutch policy

From J. V. Polišenský, "The Thirty Years' War," *Past and Present*, No. 6 (November 1954), pp. 31–42. Reprinted by permission of the author and *Past and Present*. *Past and Present*, a journal of historical studies, is obtainable from the Business Manager, *Past and Present*, Corpus Christi College, Oxford, England.

*and Bohemia (1608–1620) appeared in 1958, and during the last few years he
has published articles on Swedish and Danish policy in the 1618–1620 period.
Other studies have treated Silesia and the Thirty Years' War, the war and the
Czech people, and relations between East and West in the early years of the
war. He has also published a brief history of Czechoslovakia, an article on
Comenius, and a number of other works. There can be little doubt that he is
the leading authority of our time on the Bohemian revolt, and one of the most
productive scholars concerned with the Thirty Years' War. As the following
article will indicate, he believes that many of the traditional interpretations of
the period must be revised. Polišenský has been active, too, in the historical
profession, having served on the editorial board of a Czech historical journal
and on the advisory board of the English historical journal,* Past and Present,
where the article from which this selection is taken was published in 1954.

Polišenský has now published a book, The Thirty Years' War, *in which he
analyzes the experiences of a small Moravian town and the economic activities of landowners like Wallenstein in order to draw attention to the social
and economic forces at work on the local level during this period.*

In his stimulating work on the seventeenth century, G. N. Clark writes:

> *Somewhere about the middle of the seventeenth century European life was
> so completely transformed in many of its aspects that we commonly think
> of this as one of the great watersheds of modern history.*

Even if we cannot accept all his statements, Mr. Clark's introductory
thesis is a workable one.

The English Revolution and the Treaties of Westphalia mark the
end of a long period of transition and rapid change. This period has
so many similarities with the world we live in that more than one contemporary writer has been induced to say "we are living in the seventeenth century."

It is not our aim to discover historical parallels, but to understand
how change was brought about. But, unless we share W. Näf's de-
scription of the Thirty Years' War as the last of the religious wars and
one of the many "Kabinettkriege," we must admit that its outcome
was vitally important for the whole of continental Europe; and we
may therefore hope that a closer study of the change in society in
the seventeenth century may improve our understanding of both the
past and present troubles of the European Community.

Traditional interpretations have an unfortunate tendency towards a conservative oversimplification, and thereby inhibit historians from using new methods, as well as new sources. The Thirty Years' War is traditionally pictured as a religious conflict which "degenerated" into a political one, or as a political conflict camouflaged by religious ideologies. Traditionally it is limited in space and time, to the years 1618–1648 and to the territory of Germany and her neighbors.

This interpretation does not explain why the Dutch see the conflict as but a part of their Eighty Years' War, why the Pope sided with the Lutheran Swedes, why their victory at Breitenfeld over the Imperial Army was celebrated in Moscow with the ringing of bells, with divine services and a military parade. Italians like Romolo Quazza and Soviet historians like B. F. Porshnev and O. L. Vainstein doubt that the conflict was a predominantly German affair. Czech historians are also unsatisfied that a war which started with the coup in Prague (the defenestration of 23rd May, 1618) and ended with the fighting on the Old Bridge in Prague in October 1648 has much specifically German about it.

The most recent writer to examine the origin of the traditional interpretation [S. H. Steinberg] has stressed that it is based on two groups of documents—the official propaganda of the victorious powers, especially Sweden and Brandenburg, and on unwittingly one-sided private records of middle-class writers, who, in this author's view, are "those who suffered most." His conclusion, that the traditional view was created by the Brandenburg propagandists of the latter half of the seventeenth century and accepted by the German bourgeois historians of the nineteenth century, can, in general, be accepted.

But it must not be forgotten that the defeated side also had their historians and propagandists, strong enough to make their version an official one in central Europe for at least a century, and one that lingers even today among strictly Catholic writers. The middle-class writers certainly represent a group that suffered much, but they did not suffer most. The worst sufferers were the "Boors, the rabble, the common people." They found but few apologists, and these had little chance to challenge the official view.

The conception of the "Great German War," popularized by men of letters from Grimmelshausen . . . to Gustav Freytag, lost much of its appeal after the unification of Germany by Prussia. At the beginning of the present century, Professor R. Hoeniger and his pupils tried to show that the results of the war were far less disastrous than had been asserted before Germany became a highly militarized power. R. Hoeniger, and especially H. Preuss, representatives of the view that the war only completed the decline of Germany were severely criticized by G. Franz, the historian of the great Peasant War in Germany; Franz held that the direct results of the war were less serious than the agrarian crisis which came to a head after its conclusion. He showed that the crisis was a prolonged one, but said nothing about its origins.

Before 1933 most German historians, especially W. Goetz and W. Mommsen, abandoned the conception of the Thirty Years' War as a religious war in favor of a view that its causes were many and varied. After Hitler's accession to power, G. Ritter and W. Wostry reverted to the picture of a "belated echo of confessional struggles" which changed into a struggle for power. To this, rather illogically, Professor Ritter added the "national passions of the Czech people" as one of the causes of the war. K. Brandi also emphasized the religious motives, and it is his work which has deeply influenced the most recent English study, published by Miss C. V. Wedgwood in 1939.

Miss Wedgwood approached the difficult subject with great courage; her book reads well. But in her view the conflict was unnecessary, and seems almost meaningless. She claims impartiality, but her standpoint is heavily indebted to the writers of the Imperial party. Her bibliography cites works in nearly a dozen different languages, and, indeed, it would be difficult to produce an adequate study without at least a reading knowledge of the languages of the peoples actively involved. But a look at her scanty Czech titles suggests that they were drawn either from other bibliographies, or from works in German, or even in Spanish. The section of her book which deals with the conflict in Bohemia appears to be based almost exclusively on writings in German. She has missed modern writers like V. L. Tapié, who is well acquainted with the Czech literature, and has gone wrong over facts and arguments in the older works. It is not true that "the Estates of Bohemia consisted of three divisions, nobles, burghers and peasants," for the structure of Czech society was solidly feudal before 1618. Her authority, A. Gindely, says that Count Thurn, one of the leaders of the anti-Hapsburg revolt, was from his youth a

Protestant who spoke poor Czech. Miss Wedgwood makes him a Catholic who turned Lutheran, and knew no Czech. When she calls the Count a "mere knight," one wonders if she understands the significance of titles. When Gindely says that the Emperor left the country in charge of ten deputy-governors, Miss Wedgwood reduces them to five. Her knowledge of the linguistic character of the country is at fault. Though her work is a brave presentation of the Imperialist case, it is doubtful whether it can claim to remain "the standard authority on the subject."

The late Georges Pagès, also writing in 1939, did not represent Germany as the center of everything. He saw the Thirty Years' War as a European conflict, subtly directed by French diplomacy. This is more or less the view of Edward McCabe, who regards the war as the result of a "scramble for power" between existing political units, and within each of them.

This "scramble for power" has been put into perspective by O. L. Vainstein. "In point of fact," he writes, "the European crisis existed long before the beginning of the fighting in Germany." He seeks the beginning of this crisis in the sixteenth century . . . and specifically in the third quarter of the century, in the struggle of the United Provinces against the Spanish Hapsburgs. Vainstein regards the revolt of the Dutch as the first blow to the Hapsburg claims to hegemony. "The signal for the crisis of European (and inner German) contradictions was given by the national revolution in Bohemia."

But, though Vainstein . . . [thinks] that the Thirty Years' War was the logical outcome of a long political crisis, [he] pay[s] very little attention to the background of this crisis.

The belief that the conflict was of European dimensions was fairly common among contemporary writers. Thus two of the three speakers in the anonymous "Unpartial Discussion . . . of the Causes of the Bohemian War" of 1632, a "Bohemian" and a "Dutchman" combat the assertion of a German nobleman (a "Junker") that the preliminary part of the long conflict (the revolt of the Estates of Bohemia against the Hapsburgs, or the Bohemian War 1618–1620) was the outcome of an unnecessary and trivial revolt. In their opinion, the Bohemian nobility acted in self-defense, trying to stave off the coming onslaught of their adversaries.

The most famous of Czech writers of the period, John Amos
Comenius, addressed an eloquent plea to the Swedish Chancellor
Oxenstierna in October 1648. He stressed the fact that his countrymen, "when lately the enemies wanted to destroy all, one after another, bore the brunt of the attack, so that by their ruin they gave
others a chance to defend themselves." This argument is repeated
again and again in the diplomatic correspondence of 1618–1620. It
occurs frequently in letters sent by the King-elect of Bohemia,
Frederick of the Palatinate, to the States General. Again and again
we hear of a fight against a "danger and commotion of the whole of
Christendom," of the coming attack of the Hapsburgs against "the
whole West and these lands," of "nostre comun party."

In the diplomatic dealings between Prague, London and the Hague
other aspects of the struggle were stressed; the importance of the
economic factor and the recurring affinities between the revolt of
the United Provinces against Spain and that of the Bohemian Estates.
From February to October 1620 Sir Dudley Carleton, English Ambassador at the Hague, reported back home on the entangled problem of
Dutch subsidies for Bohemia and the Dutch requests for a prompt
settlement with London, concerning the fishing rights. Although Sir
Dudley protested that he "saw no community they (the affairs of
Germany and Bohemia) had . . . with the fishing upon the coasts of
England, Scotland and Ireland," he had to repeat similar requests for
the settlement of the Anglo-Dutch rivalry in the East Indies and upon
the coast of Greenland. The most eloquent attempt to stress the
parallels between the beginnings of the revolt in the Netherlands and
in Bohemia is found in the Ecclesiastical History of the Czech exile
Paul Skála. Sir Dudley Carleton at the Hague knew his Dutch hosts
better, explaining their willingness to aid the Bohemian rebels "as
that, which doth much import them to keep the house of Austria busy
elsewhere now towards the time of the expiration of the truce (with
Spain in 1621)."

There were many people at the beginning of the seventeenth century who were of the opinion that "the revolutions of the world will in
all likelihood before many days pass over our heads, forcibly carry
us out of this peaceable time." Since the successful revolt of the
Dutch bourgeoisie against its feudal ruler, the United Provinces was
the nucleus of a loose "party," of a predominantly Protestant group,

enemies both of the Catholic Church and the Spanish and Austrian Hapsburgs. It included the following states: England, France, the Scandinavian kingdoms, the Swiss cantons and the German princes, sometimes Venice, together with sympathizers in central and eastern Europe, among them the Protestant Estates of Bohemia and Hungary. Their opponents formed a more clearly defined and more formidable group, comprising the combined might of the "Casa d'Austria" the two branches of the Hapsburg dynasty, the Papal Curia, most of the Italian states and the "Spain of the North"—Poland. Not even Turkey and Russia were outside these two systems.

There were considerable differences among the member-states of both groups, but there were some features common to each. Thus the Protestant party comprised the "unsatisfied" powers and the Catholic party the "satisfied" powers of the sixteenth century. And while Spain, especially after 1580, had a virtual monopoly in the exploitation of colonies, the Protestants sought to break down this monopoly. At the same time Spanish claims to a universal, Catholic monarchy were supported by the authors of innumerable pamphlets. . . .

The Spanish monarchy was synonymous with the government which the Hapsburgs introduced in Castile after their defeat of the Communeros. The Spanish model of a "dominium absolutum" was accepted without reservations by the members of the Austrian branch of the Hapsburg dynasty, as well as a number of other monarchs of the "Spanish" group. The characteristic feature of this type of feudal absolute monarchy was total disregard of the interests of the smaller dependents of the feudal ruling class, especially the burgesses of the royal towns. This disregard, together with the burden of taxation, cost the Spaniards dear in the Netherlands, where a rich, rising bourgeoisie knew that the Netherlands had a key position in the realm of the Spanish Hapsburgs. Though we have today a better knowledge of the regime of Philip II the fact remains that the Hapsburgs differed from their colleagues on the French and English thrones in their attempt to eliminate the influence of the estates. It is not enough to say that "the general progress of time was towards absolutism." The trend to it coexisted at the beginning of the seventeenth century with the trend towards the representation of the economically active members of the lower nobility and bourgeoisie. We must not forget that these elements had to come into a fierce conflict with the absolutist state. Neither the absolute monarchy nor the "imperium mixtum," in which the monarchy had to share its powers with an assembly of estates, was in itself "progressive" or "retrogressive." What was important was the relation of one or the other form of state to the different social groups. The old landed class was on the defensive in an age of expanding money economy and the "price revolution." A. F. Pollard once stated that the break-up of the feudalism of the Middle Ages was the cause of the social unrest of the sixteenth century. We can go further; it certainly led to an intensified struggle for power in the state, for well paid jobs, for the control of the economic resources of the country in question, for the reintegration of burgher and peasant communities into the old order.

Only in the Netherlands, in England, and temporarily in France, was the bourgeoisie powerful enough to hold its own. In these countries, towns were flourishing centers of commerce and industry, where big capital was accumulated. In Poland, eastern Germany and partially also in the south of Europe, the towns were being incorporated into the economy of big estates (demesnes). The result was the decline of towns and a new wave of serfdom or at least of attempts to legalize the serflike conditions of the subjugation of the peasant population.

In most Continental countries political power was still in the hands of a feudal aristocracy. It is therefore necessary to study closely the devices its members used to overcome their economic difficulties. This could be done effectively either in and through the absolute monarchy or the monarchy of the estates. A considerable majority of landholders preferred the older system of estates. On the other hand, feudal monarchs found it easier to group at their courts the members of the high nobility. To their amazement they discovered, especially in central Europe, that their struggle against the opposition of the estates coincided with their attempts to defeat the religious ideology they had learned to hate, Protestantism, especially the militant form of it, Calvinism. Thus the fight against the defenders of the system of estates went hand in hand with the fight against Protestant nobility and Protestant burghers.

Thus, it appears that the political conflict, commonly called the Thirty Years' War, was the logical outcome of the crisis of policy of the old feudal ruling class. This political crisis of the declining sixteenth and the commencing seventeenth centuries had deep social and economic roots. Economic and political changes did not develop evenly. The law of uneven development resulted in a peculiar situation in those countries whose economic and political interests were in a violent contradiction. These "buffer-countries" lay in a disputed no-man's land and were necessarily regarded as natural danger zones.

The case of Bohemia, where the conflict broke out in the end [typifies] . . . the contradictions inside and uneven development of the economic basis of a given society, its ideas and institutions. . . .

If we want to elucidate the causes of the conflict, to explain why the conflict had started in Bohemia, and not in the Rhineland or in the Danubian area, we must have in mind the actual situation the lands of the Crown of Bohemia (Bohemia proper, Moravia, Silesia and Lusatia) were in at the beginning of the seventeenth century. From 1526 they were part of the multinational realm of the Austrian Hapsburgs. In that monarchy these lands had a key position. They paid more taxes and sent more soldiers against the Turks than any other possessions of the Hapsburgs. At the time, when three of the Electors of the Empire were staunch Catholics and the three others equally staunch Protestants, the Bohemian vote secured the Imperial dignity for the Hapsburgs.

This important position found Bohemia (we will thus refer to the four lands of the Crown of Bohemia) extraordinarily ill-equipped. What was the position of Bohemia in the changing society of the late sixteenth century?

Although the Hussite movement of the fifteenth century had up to that time been the worst blow the feudal order ever suffered, it did not destroy that order. The position of the old feudal ruling class had been seriously impaired but it was not destroyed. On the contrary, very soon the landlords began a swift counter-attack to regain most of their lost positions. Peasants were in a better position in the Bohemia of the fifteenth century than anywhere else in central Europe. When the landlords attempted to subdue the peasant masses, the peasants defended their "old liberties." They lost most of them by the beginning of the seventeenth century, but the process of commutation of the labor rent into a money rent was still going on and feudal demesnes dependent on servile labor were relatively few. Much greater was the number of demesnes using wage labor. The peasants in the grain-growing areas were not yet excluded from the market. Though there were numerous conflicts between peasants and their overlords, collective resistance or risings were relatively few before 1618.

Bohemian towns also gained many valuable privileges during the Hussite wars, but they too suffered from the renewed offensive of the feudal forces of society. . . . The knights were either joining the ranks of the nobles or rapidly losing their land. They were usually considered the backbone of the lower nobility, because the old difference between them had long since disappeared. Their number was rapidly diminishing, and many of them were in a dependent position as stewards of big lords or officers of the Crown. What is even more important, there were hardly any yeomen left in Bohemia, and such as there were, they were without money and influence. With small landlords disappearing and hardly a nucleus of rural bourgeoisie in existence, the magnates ruled in the countryside.

General uncertainty stimulated the more active of the feudal lords to a feverish economic activity. Diminishing incomes rather than anything else were its cause. This was also the source of animosity against the townspeople, which led the nobles to their actual betrayal in 1547, when a rising against the Hapsburgs failed and the towns were made to pay dearly for their temerity. They lost their political influence and their economic privileges and could not defend themselves against ruthless exploitation by the King and the aristocracy. The heavy burden of taxation and forced loans bled the towns white. . . . English, and other foreign merchants (especially merchants from Nuremberg, Vienna and Italy) had in their hands the most important branches of trade and industry. Even the Prague patriciate only exceptionally took part in mining (copper, zinc, tin) while the developing linen industry with its elements of dispersed manufacture was in the hands of foreigners. Thus the export of manufactured goods fell at a time when the old basis of the country's wealth, the Bohemian silver mines, lost their importance in view of cheaper American silver. The old mining centers, Jáchymov (Joachimsthal) and Kutná Hora in Bohemia, Rychleby in Silesia declined, while the era of iron had not yet started. Here, too, the initiative was in the hands of the Crown, the magnates and the foreigners, mostly from the Netherlands. Thus the economic life of Bohemia round 1600 shows serious signs of shrinkage of production and markets.

Bohemia, the economic backbone of the power of the Austrian Hapsburgs was economically a weak country with the dangerous reputation of being a rich country. Aspects of the economic malaise explain the growing intensity of the struggle for power. Together with nine tenths of the population, a large majority of the nobility and nearly all the townspeople were Protestant of different shades. They were also defenders of the old political "liberties" against the Hapsburgs. The minority of the ruling class formed the "Spanish" party at the court. Their hope lay in a speedy victory of the Hapsburg ruler. In the same year 1609, when the Dutch signed a twelve years' truce with the Spaniard, the Bohemian Estates gained a temporary victory over their opponents in the famous Letter of Majesty, guaranteeing their religious liberties. A new constitution for the country was also prepared, but it was never agreed to by the Hapsburgs. On the contrary, in 1617 the combined strength of the Spanish and the Austrian branches of the Hapsburg family forced the Estates to accept Ferdinand II as their future King. The "Spanish" party, now in power, started a campaign against their opponents, and these, reckoning on the approaching renewal of hostilities on the Netherlands front, tried to anticipate the coming onslaught. This led to the "defenestration" and the opening of hostilities.

In the light of the new sources the course of the conflict can also be corrected. With Germany and Bohemia as principal battlegrounds, with England leaving the conflict long before the outbreak of the Civil War, with Sweden, fighting with Dutch, French and Russian subsidies, and France waiting for her chance, only the Netherlands and the Hapsburgs stayed on as permanent dramatis personae. Brussels and the Hague formed for the most part (especially in the earlier stages of the conflict) the axis of all diplomatic activity. And if the Dutch failed to help the Bohemian Estates in 1618–1620, if they were at the same time active as bankers and industrial organizers in both Sweden and Denmark, if they deserted the coalition in January 1648, all this can be explained by the inner development of the model

capitalist country of the seventeenth century. Similarly the final abandonment of the Bohemian cause by the allies was closely connected
with the situation in Sweden.

The economic interests of the De Geer family are visible wherever
copper was known to be buried under the ground. But neither the
generals, nor the diplomatic agents, not even early capitalists like De
Geer, are the heroes of the war. These are to be seen in the common
people, tortured, robbed and wantonly murdered by soldiery of both
sides. As early as 1620, the foreign "observers," then present with
the Bohemian army, the Dutch van Mario, the Venetian agent Carlo
Antonini and the English agent Francis Nethersole wrote in the same
vein of the great peasant risings in the rear of both armies. In the
end, they say, one cannot blame the poor "boers," they have already
suffered too much. And that was only the beginning of the war! These
popular movements, whether in Moravia, southern Italy, Germany or
Normandy, resembling the risings of the Clubmen of the West Country
during the Civil War, are indispensable to a realistic picture of the
conflict.

There is a lot to be said about the consequences of the war. The
treaties of Westphalia found England too busy with her internal
affairs. The Dutch had their independence guaranteed and the danger
of the Spanish "universal monarchy" disappeared, but the Austrian
Hapsburgs, though virtually pushed out of Germany, got a carte
blanche in central and southeastern Europe. In this area the consequences of the treaties were fatal. It meant victory for the political
and ideological program of the Hapsburgs, together with the program
of a restored feudal order. In most parts of central Europe, especially
in Bohemia, this meant an interruption of former development and
a wholesale destruction of material and cultural assets accumulated
by generations. Hussite Bohemia ceased to exist in the middle of the
seventeenth century and was followed by the Bohemia of the "second
serfdom," which decided that even the future development towards
capitalism would bring few positive assets to the country and the
people.

A historian, looking back over the space of three centuries at the
peculiar exhibition of power politics, called the Thirty Years' War,
cannot but conclude that this war, like the poverty and the disease

that accompanied it, was a morbid phenomenon signalizing a break-down in the process of civilization. It would be utterly false to glorify this military conflict, caused by a political crisis, which was itself the outcome of social and economic changes taking place in a period of transition.

Theodore K. Rabb

THE ECONOMIC EFFECTS OF THE WAR REVIEWED

Prejudices and uncertainties have constantly obstructed scholars who have tried to estimate the effects of the Thirty Years' War on Germany. There is still little agreement about the state of the German economy during the half-century before 1618, and even less about the economic effects of the war. There has been a long controversy surrounding this problem, and a great deal of evidence has been uncovered. This article outlines the main features and results of the dispute.

The view that the Thirty Years' War was a crippling economic blow was traditional from the time of Samuel von Pufendorf, the court historian of the Great Elector of Brandenburg, until the late nineteenth century. It was then challenged by a number of historians who contended that Germany was already in an economic decline before 1618 and that the war was only the final blow to a tottering economy. Often repeated and persuasively argued, this became the widely accepted theory. But later there was again a reaction among specialists, and since then opinions have remained divided. There have thus been two main theories, or schools. The first, which considers Germany prosperous until wrecked by the war, may be named the "di-

From Theodore K. Rabb, "The Effects of the Thirty Years' War on the German Economy," *The Journal of Modern History* 34 (March 1962): 40–51. Reprinted by permission of the editors of *The Journal of Modern History* and the University of Chicago Press. Copyright 1962 by The University of Chicago.

sastrous war" school. The second, which usually does not deny that the war was a calamity, but claims that it was only the final blow in a deteriorating situation, can be called the "earlier decline" school. Before examining the views of the two sides in detail, however, their usage of certain fundamental terms and concepts requires clarification.

First, despite the enormous differences between the various sections of Germany in the seventeenth century, the country is regarded as an economic entity. But the patent absence of any economic unity between, for instance, the areas east and west of the Elbe, makes the "entity" an artificial creation. References to "general" conditions must therefore be viewed as applying to a majority of the separate areas within Germany rather than to any all-embracing whole. Second, the effect of the war on German culture is frequently brought into the discussion, even though this is a separate problem, bearing no palpable relation to the controversy about economics. A similar view must be taken of the introduction of political conditions as evidence or reasons for economic trends. Here again distinctions must not be blurred. Undoubtedly, Germany was politically on the downgrade, but the effects of this situation on economics are uncertain: although enmities, diversities, and disunity did hamper economic activity, the local rivalries of the princes led to much governmental encouragement of trade and industry. The many references to political conditions must therefore fall largely outside the scope of the discussion that follows.

Finally, there has been a tendency to confuse relative and absolute trends. Causes of German decline are often cited without the qualification that they refer to a decline that existed only in relation to the greater growth of other countries, such as England and Holland, after the mid-sixteenth century. Too rarely is it realized that retrogression in *absolute* terms is a different matter, since the eclipse of spectacular achievements did not necessarily affect the steady prosperity below. Proof of relative decline must therefore not be seen as an argument against absolute prosperity.

The controversy has passed through three main stages: from its start to roughly 1910; from 1910 to World War II; and from World War

II to the present. It began in reaction to the novelist Gustav Freytag, who presented in 1861, in a vivid and widely read book *(Aus dem Jahrhundert des grossen Krieges),* an extreme form of the traditional view that a vicious Thirty Years' War descended upon a happy and prosperous Germany. . . . He luridly described the war, largely from the pages of Christopher von Grimmelshausen's semifanciful account, *Simplicissimus,* first published in 1669. The opposite view, that Germany had been declining before 1618, was rare, but had some support.

Eventually a few German historians began to consider the necessity of refuting Freytag's book, which, with its wide circulation and presentation of an extreme picture, had popularized the traditional view in an absurdly overstated form. Moreover, it had easily gained wide acceptance at a time of growing German nationalism, since it proclaimed the view that foreigners could be blamed for Germany's economic backwardness in the seventeenth century. The scholarly world, however, left Freytag unchallenged for over twenty-five years, probably because his views had been corroborated, in a milder way, by the distinguished historian Karl Theodor von Inama-Sternegg. When the reaction came, these two, Freytag and Inama Sternegg, became the symbols of the traditional "disastrous war" theory. They were the main targets of the stream of refutations which characterized the first stage of the controversy.

The first detailed refutation appeared in 1886. Presented by Eberhard Gothein, its basic arguments were to be repeated by most of its successors. In brief, Gothein believed that the Thirty Years' War was blamed for a decline that had set in long before, because of restrictions, feuds, political and religious chaos, and basic disunity—all good reasons but not evidence. To bolster his case, he drew examples from his studies of the upper Rhine Valley. He did not think that the exceptions he found, such as the prosperous cattle farmers in the Black Forest, qualified his general thesis at all. Nor did he differentiate between absolute and relative trends. Though a pioneer of the "early decline" theory, he, too, was an ardent German nationalist, believing that only when Germany was united could she flourish. The inconsistency of stressing German disunity, yet generalizing from evidence from a limited area, was one that many of his successors had in common with Gothein. Within six years a general history appeared that accepted Gothein's refutations, and thereafter the "earlier decline" school gathered strength.

During the first decade of the twentieth century important contributions came from Robert Hoeniger and Georg von Below, who followed Gothein's lead and attacked Freytag. The former thought that, because of disunity, the prosperity of some areas could not help Germany as a whole. But he did not mention the possibility that the decline of some areas might also not affect Germany as a whole. He saw signs of a late sixteenth-century decline in the collapse of the Hanseatic League and of the great south German bankers and their mines, and in the appearance of national states. The war itself he considered beneficial in some ways, because it helped the peasants and created a German military spirit, but he did point out that regional studies were needed if substantial conclusions were to be made. His call for local research was of supreme importance. Without these studies, which have come in abundance since Hoeniger's article, the whole problem today, fifty years later, would still be uncertain and burdened by unfounded generalizations. Below was more moderate but, basing his ideas on his studies of Jülich-Berg, he gave powerful support to the "earlier decline" school. He, too, regarded lightly the exceptions to the general decline. It is interesting that, as a medievalist, he could not resist the temptation to take causes, in this case restrictions on trade, back to the Middle Ages.

Below considered two of his contemporaries in need of criticism. One, Berthold Haendcke, had come to the conclusion that even the early seventeenth century was a flourishing period for German culture, yet he had taken the anti-Freytag line on the economy. It was the former conclusion to which Below objected. Another writer, Hugo Preuss, had taken Gothein's thesis too far. Preuss considered the German economy to have been in decline ever since the early sixteenth century: the bankers had kept their money to themselves, or had lent it to foreigners and had therefore not helped their native Germany. The views of both Haendcke and Preuss were obviously colored by strong national feelings.

The various rebuttals of Freytag that dominated the first stage of the controversy were summarized a little later in a general work by

Karl Lamprecht. But the local evidence that was being amassed on both sides was still inconclusive. . . .

Despite the scanty support of local evidence, the "earlier decline" school remained dominant for a long time, though it was opposed in works which dealt with the problem as a whole. Dietrich Schäfer, the author of the first complete attack on the newly accepted trend, wrote his major work in 1910, the date which has therefore been chosen as the opening of the second stage of the controversy.

Without resorting to Freytag's methods, Schäfer concluded in a general history of Germany that the country was not declining on the eve of the Thirty Years' War. He had written an article thirteen years previously in which he had pointed out that the changing trade routes of the world had not necessarily caused a German economic decline. In his larger work, he extended his treatment to a discussion of the entire problem of the German economy. Drawing on local studies, he presented a telling case against the "earlier decline" school. He admitted that there had been a relative decline, but in absolute terms he saw the period as a time of advance. He was the first to make this distinction; and although he did not have quite enough facts to support his generalizations, he made a most important contribution to the controversy.

The second stage, lasting until World War II, was the most active period of the dispute. For clarity's sake, one can divide the literature into four categories: works which were concerned with the dispute as a whole; regional or detailed studies; writings which threw light on the problem though not specifically dealing with it; and books on wider subjects, which referred to the problem only in passing. The latter can serve as an indication of the relative degree of acceptance of the two main theories among nondisputants.

During the "second generation" of the controversy, four scholars in particular made attempts to reach a solution of the problem. First, from Johann Friedrick Dürr, came two articles. In the earlier of these he argued that the war did bring severe destruction to prosperous areas, and that the accounts of contemporaries, though certainly exaggerated, had a considerable basis in fact. His evidence was drawn from the town of Heilbronn, which in general seemed to support his contention. Using some new local studies . . . , he argued that many areas of Germany were prosperous until hit by the war. In the second article he admitted that some places were declining before 1618, but added that even to them the war was a crippling disaster.

The opposing view of the problem was taken by Fritz Kaphahn in two articles. The first showed that, largely because of their continued extravagance despite declining production, the credit of German towns was ruined by 1600; their organization then collapsed during the war. In the second, Kaphahn revealed his general views. He noted various exceptions, such as the rise of the landed gentry east of the Elbe, and the growth of German Baltic trade as revealed by the Sound dues;[1] but in general he thought the country was declining because of complacency and falling production, stressing particularly the vast debts incurred before 1618. But he failed to distinguish between relative and absolute decline: a "sign" of general decline was that Baltic trade was growing more rapidly than Germany's part in it.

Oswald Redlich wrote only one article on the subject, but it is interesting because it presented the first full statement of the view that the war actually benefited Germany. Reviewing only some of the local studies, he concluded that the "earlier decline" theory was correct and contended that the war was a help to Germany because it cleared the way for a rapid, constructive, and much-needed recovery in the late seventeenth century. The latter argument may be true, and it is a neat complement to the "earlier decline" theory, but it is irrelevant to the controversy.

The last important contribution of this period was made by Theodor Mayer. He supported the "disastrous war" school, although in an early article he did agree that the destruction caused by the war paved the way for the emergence of a state economy in Germany. His major study was a survey of the literature and an attempt at a balanced view. He first put forward the idea that the loss of some areas might have been the gain of others. He argued more convincingly than anyone to date that Germany was prospering in 1618. He pointed out that trade continued to grow despite the downfall of the Hanseatic League and that the collapse of the great capitalists was no evidence for general decline, since their cities still prospered.

[1] These were tolls paid by all ships which passed through the only entrance to the Baltic, a strait known as the Sound.—Ed.

But he overstressed his own views. In particular, he failed to realize that there had been a decline relative to other European countries.

The most important advance made during this second stage of the controversy was the steady accumulation of regional research. There is space here to record only the various conclusions. Of thirty-four studies made between 1910 and 1943 that have been examined, twenty-four supported the "disastrous war" school, and only ten the "earlier decline" school. It is also worth noting that a series of local histories in the *Monographien Deutscher Städte,* published in Berlin in the 1920s and 1930s and covering such towns as Coburg, Fulda, and Nördlingen, further supported the "disastrous war" school. None of them maintained that the war came only as a final blow to towns already in the grip of decline. In this they supported the more detailed studies . . . which . . . stressed that the war started a decline when it came to various prosperous areas in Germany. These studies were not equally comprehensive or important, and further research may show that the balance seems weighted too heavily in favor of the "disastrous war" school. Yet there does not seem to be enough material still available for the balance to be seriously altered. Thus it seems difficult to escape the conclusion that, within Germany, more areas were gaining than losing prosperity in the prewar years. Decline seems to have been widespread only in the wake of the war. . . . [Yet], despite the lack of certainty among specialists, the general works that appeared during this second stage were overwhelmingly in favor of the "earlier decline" theory.[2]

[2] R. Kötzschke, *Grundzüge der deutschen Wirtschaftsgeschichte bis zur 17. Jahrhunderts* (Leipzig, 1923), supported "earlier decline." So did F. Bülow, *Volkswirtschaftslehre* (Leipzig, 1934), where all the arguments to "prove" decline were arrayed; they ranged from the fall of Constantinople to German political difficulties. But he argued against himself when he said that the new trade routes took spices away from declining Nuremberg and Augsburg, yet instead brought them to Frankfurt am Main. Here the problems involved in calling Germany an economic entity become obvious. C. V. Wedgwood, *The Thirty Years War* (London, 1938), also joined the "earlier decline" school, though she did regard the war as responsible for the virtual disintegration of society. If she dealt with the problem rapidly, then two other non-Germans slipped past it at astonishing speed: D. Ogg, *Europe in the 17th Century* (London, 1925), cast only a contemptuous look at German culture before the war; and G. Pagès, *La Guerre de Trente Ans* (Paris, 1939), mentioned only the prewar political chaos, though he did say that prosperity *returned* after 1648. J. Haller, *Die Epochen der deutschen Geschichte* (Stuttgart, 1943), writing at a time of excessive nationalist feeling, clearly accepted the "earlier decline" theory, blaming German disunity not on home-grown, beneficial Lutheranism, but on disruptive foreign movements: Calvinism and the Counter Reformation.

It might be well to mention here the particularly difficult problem of the effects of the war on Germany's population. Though constantly discussed during the dispute, and closely related to the economic situation, trends in population are themselves a complex subject, and full treatment would require a separate article. The most important work has been done by scholars not involved in the more general controversy, so here only these leading contributions and a few current conclusions will be mentioned.

Estimates of population changes during the war have ranged from a drop of two-thirds, considered credible by Inama-Sternegg, to a drop of at most 5 percent, according to Hoeniger. The most acceptable treatment, because the most widely based on local research, was by Günther Franz. He stressed the fact that generalization is impossible, since different areas had very different experiences. He discussed the regional variations, such as the stagnation in the northwest and the decline in the northeast, and concluded that the average loss over all Germany was between 30 and 40 percent. His figures were accepted by Roger Mols in the most recent full survey of the problem.

According to Franz and Mols, there now seems to be enough evidence to state that, despite regional variations, the war was a disaster for Germany's population. Mols pointed out that a few towns did manage to grow in size because of migrations, but he considered these rare exceptions. He concluded that even in the areas of Germany least harmed "la guerre réussit à y enrayer les progrès en cours depuis le XVIe siècle." Such a conclusion, based on widespread evidence, undermined any support that population trends might have given to the "earlier decline" theory. But if they are instead to support the "disastrous war" school, then prewar population figures are also needed. For these figures one must look to the valuable contribution of Gustav Schmoller.

Schmoller gathered numerous statistics, but found it impossible to generalize about a country whose areas and cities differed so much. In the fifty years or so before 1618 Leipzig grew while Cologne shrank, Nuremberg expanded but Magdeburg contracted, and so on. Yet one interesting conclusion can be drawn from his figures: hardly any city that had been growing in 1618 increased its population between 1618 and 1648. With very few exceptions a city during the war at best stagnated, like Strassburg, or at worst shrunk by 96 percent, as did Magdeburg. In other words, although in some cities the war merely hastened a decline already in progress, in many others it ended a period of growth. Before 1618, therefore, there was both gain and loss in population, with neither predominant. After 1618, however, as Franz and Mols confirmed, there were only losses and no gains. The war therefore changed a situation of diversity into one of decline. If population trends are indications of general economic tendencies, then in this case they support the "disastrous war" school.

The period since World War II has seen a revival of the dispute, following a twenty-year lull after Mayer's contribution. With no satisfactory solution, further discussion was needed, and the renewed interest has come from England and America.

First, from S. H. Steinberg, came a new approach to the war itself. A few earlier scholars had thought that the war was of some benefit to Germany in clearing the way for the future. Yet they had also noted its various harmful effects. Steinberg's argument that the war was beneficial had far fewer qualifications. A vital part of his argument was that the foundations of the prosperity of the towns had gone by 1618, and that they were finally ruined by the inflation of 1619–1623. In fact, neither of these points can be substantiated. It has been shown above that many towns were growing in prosperity before 1618. Moreover, almost all the local studies dated the start of a decline, or intensification of decline, from the time when troops first appeared in an area, and not from 1619 or 1623. The occasional economic activity brought by troops, or the migrations that helped some regions, were rare war benefits, and for each example of such a benefit there were many more of destruction. Steinberg also claimed that the transference of property to more enterprising and productive owners, once the towns did suffer, gave Germany a greater economic potential in 1648 than in 1618. At best this was a vague, distant, and uncertain benefit, which cannot mitigate the conclusion that the direct, immediate effects of the war were not beneficial. Although the armies were small, they could be most destructive, even if they did not stay long in one area: not many days or men were needed to sack Magdeburg, an event that hardly contributed to Germany's prosperity, regardless of how many old restrictions were swept away along with most of its population. Certainly, the war's harmful effects have been exaggerated and its benefits rarely noticed. But it was primarily destructive, and Steinberg's basic premise that a nadir was reached in 1623 is not supported by the evidence. . . .

A short article by Francis L. Carsten . . . presented new evidence and also some interesting new ideas. He raised the possibility that a general decline of the towns, even if certain, was no proof of Germany's decline, because prosperity moved to the countryside. The nobles were replacing townsmen as the great traders, particularly in Prussia. He also emphasized the fact that Germany was not an economic entity. Finally, to stress the scarcity of evidence, he gave alcohol tax figures for Bavaria which he said were the best items of real evidence available. They did not reveal a decline before 1618. Despite its brevity, his article brought a new approach to the dispute. If his argument that prosperity was growing in the German countryside is not here pursued, it is because most of the evidence available is from towns; and, in any case, it does not seem to indicate a general decline. There may well have been growth relative to the towns in the countryside, yet also absolute prosperity within the towns.

The latest specialist opinion is a chapter by G. D. Ramsay in volume IV of *The new Cambridge modern history*. Carefully avoiding unfounded generalizations, Ramsay points out that not all the princes were engaged in destructive rivalries. There were some enlightened rulers, and many areas enjoyed considerable prosperity. The widespread examples he cites back his conclusion that there are no signs of general decline.

Regional studies have continued to grow in favor of the "disastrous war" school. Three that have recently appeared, as well as Carsten's study of Bavaria, have concluded that there was no pre-1618 decline. General works, however, have carefully followed their predecessors. . . .

Here, then, the dispute now stands. One hundred years after Freytag's book appeared, and despite recent renewed interest, the controversy still seems to have reached no satisfactory conclusion. Yet in fact one enormous advance has been made: the accumulation of regional research. At last some facts to support generalizations are available. Perhaps they can lead to a conclusion which has evidence and not abstraction as its basis.

The attempt to see either prosperity or decline as a *uniform* condition in Germany before 1618 has been a major stumbling block in most approaches to the problem. The absence of unity in Germany and the different conclusions reached by local studies make generalizations about the economic situation before the war virtually impossible. There was undeniably a decline in relation to some European nations, yet the "earlier decline" writers have established little more than this. The difficulty is to generalize about the absolute condition of the economy.

The survey of regional research in the previous pages makes this difficulty obvious. For it shows both absolute prosperity and decline within Germany: often side by side, and one town might prosper at the expense of its neighbor. The important revelation is that both of these economic conditions were present to such a wide extent that neither of the two can be singled out as the dominant one. Though at present local studies show much more economic growth than shrinkage before 1618, there were still many areas of decline, and some which have not been covered. So we must resist the outright generalization that prosperity was the prevalent tendency. Yet the evidence will support the contention that, before 1618, at best prosperity was dominant in Germany, and at worst there was merely diversity—coexistence of growth and decline. The fact that areas of decline were in a decided minority, however, makes it impossible to conclude that the situation before 1618 was any worse than diverse.

After 1618 there was a significant change. As the war successively struck various sections of Germany, it drastically reduced the number of prosperous areas. Economic growth became so rare a phenomenon that at last it is possible to conclude that decline was the prevalent condition. From a condition of, at worst, diversity, Germany had sunk into a situation dominated by decline. Population figures present a similar picture in a much clearer form. Whatever the long-term effects of the war, therefore, its direct, immediate effects were destructive. At best, the Thirty Years' War started a general decline that had not previously existed; at worst, it replaced prosperity with disaster.

Josef Pekař

THE TURNING-POINT IN CZECH HISTORY

Josef Pekař (1870–1937), professor of history at the University of Prague, was the foremost Czech nationalist historian of the generation following Gindely. After writing his doctoral thesis on Wallenstein (published in 1895), he turned to an earlier period of Bohemian history, and produced an important work on Jan Hus. After various other books on early Bohemia and one on economic developments in the seventeenth and eighteenth centuries, Pekař emerged in World War I as a leading anti-Austrian propagandist. Further historical works then appeared: one on the World War, another on St. Wenceslaus, a Czech national hero; various general works on Czech history; and a monumental four-volume biography of Hus's follower, Jan Žižka, another national hero. He rarely strayed far from his nationalistic concerns, and he remained involved in political issues, publishing in 1923 an attack on land reform proposals. The selection that follows comes from magazine articles Pekař wrote to commemorate the tercentenaries of the outbreak of the Bohemian revolt and the defeat at the White Mountain. They were collected together in a book published in 1921 entitled White Mountain. *The selection from Pekař's work on Wallenstein in this book comes from the enlarged revision of his doctoral thesis published first in Czech in 1934, and then in German in 1937. There, as in all his writings, the nationalism breaks through, and it is interesting that Pekař, like Gindely before him, took a poor view of Wallenstein. The condemnation of the general was in fact linked to the Bohemian cause, though this has, in turn, provoked the criticism that Pekař anachronistically spoke of a national feeling that did not yet exist.*

Today it is three hundred years. . . . On this day, whose dark shadow has been cast across three centuries, thousands of Czechs have learned to pause, their thoughts filled with sorrow. . . . In narrow prison cells, suffering as exiles, in despair over the loss of their homeland and the humiliation of their nation, their thoughts have returned to the day that is to blame. . . . This . . . painful recrimination . . . is of course a result of the ever-present memory of the sequence of events: after the 23rd of May came the White Mountain and then repeated White Mountains. . . . What interests us is . . . whether the White Mountain was a necessary consequence of the 23rd of May, 1618. Did the Czech resistance contain the seeds of

From Joseph Pekař, *Bílá Hora* (Prague, 1921), 7, 37, 41–43, 46–47, 89–90, 99–100, 107 and 158–159. (I am most grateful to my father for providing the translation from the Czech.—Ed.)

its own failure from the very start? Is it right to place on the heads of the initiators all blame for the destruction? . . . We cannot agree to a verdict of guilty against the originators of Czech resistance. . . . It is certain that the catastrophe started almost a century before, when the German religion [Lutheranism] entered the country. Before 1618 it was already impossible to avoid depending on the Germans. . . . Without a doubt the mistake was that the leaders of resistance placed too much confidence in their coreligionists. . . . This shows how religion overwhelmed all other considerations. . . .

It is said that the Czechs capitulated shamefully after one short battle. But let us not forget that this battle was preceded by a war lasting two years. . . . They could not conduct such a long war. . . . For one year, possibly two, they might have managed to keep going . . . but then, without foreign support, it became impossible. . . . Above all they lacked the spirit that could have faced the danger, that could have inspired enthusiasm, sacrifice and perseverance. . . . Their society was possibly as lazy and materialistic as at any time in our history. What a difference from the time of the Hussites! Where before national society at all levels, including the conscientious peasant, had trembled with the desire to act and to sacrifice, a society militant through and through, whose basic types in countless variations were the hero and the martyr, now there was a people spiritually complacent, thanks to easy wealth and worldly ideals, . . . concerned only with their well-being, and avoiding military service and the shedding of blood as never before. . . . One must ask where their deep religious devotion came from. . . . It seems that there was a need for the Lord Almighty largely because he could intervene when they became incapable of action. He was to help when the human being lacked the will to help himself! . . .

Yet this evaluation . . . should not mislead us. Alongside [Protestantism] . . . there fought and was finally defeated the principle of moral self-determination, that is, the principle of liberty. . . . In essence the war was a product of the fear that conscience would be forced, an act of defense against the Counter Reformation embodied by Ferdinand II. . . .

On the White Mountain the [Catholics] did not really win. However high the domes of Baroque churches and the ornate facades of Baroque palaces might later soar toward heaven as a symbol of victory in a Catholicized Prague, this symbol could never erase the memory of the tears and blood with which the brutal conqueror flooded the oppressed country in the years of humiliation. . . .

The fluctuations of fortune during the Thirty Years' War had two effects: they repeatedly offered the conquered Czech soul the hope that the day of revenge for the White Mountain was not too far distant, and they completely thwarted the plans of the agents of the Counter Reformation. During the last third of the war in particular, when time and again Swedish troops entered the country, it was impossible even to speak of conversion of peasants to the Catholic faith. Thus the last and decisive drive against Protestant believers began only after 1648, after the Peace of Westphalia had shown that the White Mountain really was the last word, that pre-White Mountain Bohemia, deserted by her allies, was going to become completely the spoil of the victor. After 1648 the Counter Reformation began in earnest. . . .

One cannot blame the destruction of Bohemia entirely on the White Mountain. The guilt rests on the conscience of the Thirty Years' War. Bohemia had already suffered considerably . . . before the White Mountain and she was devastated thereafter: villages burned, towns destroyed, widespread looting, fields left untilled. . . . It seems, however, that such a wealthy country would have recovered from the horrors and destruction of the early war years had not repeated new wars and invasions by foreign armies rendered fruitless all efforts to recover. . . . The final result of this constant frustration of attempts at recovery was that it took three generations to restore the economic condition of the country after the war. . . .

One will understand the White Mountain better if it is seen not only as a Czech but also as a central European phenomenon. . . . Yet for us it surely has a special, much deeper meaning. The difference to us lies in the fact that, after the Peace of Westphalia, Germany could revive with the help of Dutch and English influence, which slowly brought to life progressive elements latent in Protestantism. What a tragedy that this should have happened partly because of a Czech contribution: the Czech spirit emanating from the writings of the Czech exile, Comenius! But Bohemia was stifled by Jesuit censorship and the regulation of culture that the Jesuits thought necessary in face of dangers from abroad, when their best safeguard was in fact the weariness and exhaustion of Bohemia. Another difference was that in Germany all the vulgar and cowardly elements to be found in the poisoned theological and religious controversies were, so to speak, able to explode and be consumed during the long war. This showed that, notwithstanding the loss of Bohemia, beliefs cannot be suppressed by force. . . . But in Bohemia the White Mountain prolonged the war over culture and religion by more than three centuries. . . . The difference in religion acquired nationalistic and political importance for both the Czechs and the Germans only because of the conditions created by the White Mountain, of which the most significant was the end of Czech Independence. The Counter Reformation severed Bohemia and Moravia from all spiritual community with northern Germany. From this point of view one can go on to say that for us the advantage of the White Mountain was that it thoroughly and permanently split the German world (and possibly also prevented the establishment of a large German-Protestant Empire in the seventeenth century, in which Bohemia would have been included). It made German national unification impossible, and thus indirectly laid the foundation for the later emergence of Austria and so on. If we continued our investigation along these lines we might come to understand with some certainty the politico-national advantages of the White Mountain, in addition, of course . . . to the birth of Czech nationalism out of the humiliation and degradation of the White Mountain. But . . . there is no sense to this kind of assessment unless it is in answer to the question of whether the great catastrophe did not also have its good side. That it was a catastrophe, a catastrophe without measure or limit, I do not have to emphasize.

II INTERPRETATIONS OF LEADING PARTICIPANTS

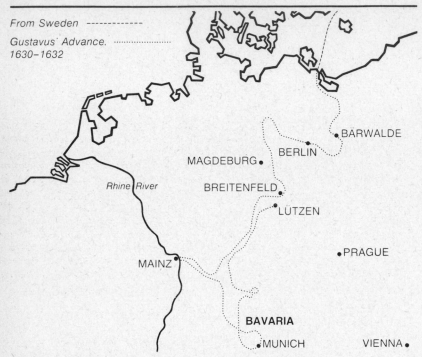

Gustavus' March through Germany, 1630–1632

From Sweden ------------

Gustavus' Advance. ....
1630–1632

BÄRWALDE

BERLIN

MAGDEBURG

Rhine River

BREITENFELD

LÜTZEN

PRAGUE

MAINZ

BAVARIA

MUNICH   VIENNA

FIGURE 3. Map of Gustavus' March through Germany, 1630–1632.

Gustavus Adolphus

Gustavus Adolphus and Axel Oxenstierna

STATEMENTS OF INTENT

*Gustavus Adolphus, king of Sweden from 1611 to 1632, is his country's na-
tional hero. In his brief reign he transformed a small, powerless, poor kingdom
into one of the arbiters of Europe, a dominant force in continental affairs.
At the same time, together with his able chief minister, Axel Oxenstierna
(1583–1654), he created the most efficient governmental administration in
Europe. Yet it is for his dazzling campaigns in Germany that he is best remembered—the military genius who destroyed the advance of Hapsburg and
Catholic once and for all. The selections which follow wrestle with the question of his motivation, but first it might be advisable to assess the few scraps
of evidence we have in which either he or Oxenstierna made explicit statements about the reasons for invading Germany. The first two extracts are
from speeches Gustavus made in Sweden in 1629, and the third is from a
statement Oxenstierna made to the government of Brandenburg in 1631.*

I

Gustavus. Denmark is used up. The Papists are on the Baltic,
they have Rostock, Wismar, Stettin, Wolgast, Griefswald, and nearly
all the other ports in their hands; Rügen is theirs, and from Rügen
they continue to threaten Stralsund; their whole aim is to destroy
Swedish commerce, and soon to plant a foot on the southern shore
of our Fatherland. Sweden is in danger from the power of the Hapsburg; that is all, but it is enough; that power must be met, swiftly and
strongly. The times are bad; the danger is great. It is no time to ask
whether the cost will not be far beyond what we can bear. The fight
will be for parents, for wife and child, for house and home, for Fatherland and Faith.

The first two selections are taken from C. R. L. Fletcher, *Gustavus Adolphus and the
Thirty Years' War* (London, 1890; paperback edition, New York, 1963), pp. 97–98; the
third selection is from Michael Roberts, ed., *Sweden as a Great Power, 1611–1697*
(New York, 1968), p. 139.

II

Gustavus. I did not call you [the royal Council] together because I had any doubt in my mind, but in order that you might enjoy the freedom of opposing me if you wished. That freedom you can no longer enjoy; you have spoken. My view is this: that, for our safety, honor, and final peace, I see nothing but a bold attack on the enemy. I hope that it will be for the advantage of Sweden, but I also hope that, if the day go hard with us, no blame will be laid upon me, for I have no other end in view but that advantage. I do not underrate the difficulties—such as the want of means, the doubtful issue of the battle; in which it is no idle glory that I am seeking—the King of Denmark is a sufficient warning to me against that—besides the judgment of posterity generally leaves a man very little glory. And I am satisfied with glory, and want no more. Your duty is clear; to exhort all my subjects to continue in their present devoted attitude. I hereby advise you so to bear yourselves, and all over whom you have influence, that either you or your children may live to see a good end of this matter; which may the Most High grant.

III

Oxenstierna. [The King's intention's] were, in general, to disrupt the plans of the enemy, whose proceedings and intentions with regard to the Baltic are sufficiently well known. His Majesty therefore intended to ensure the safety of his kingdom and the Baltic, and to liberate oppressed [German] lands; and thereafter to proceed according as events might develop: it was no part of his original intention to press on as far as he did. . . . The King would have adapted his policies in the light of the enemy's action, the circumstances of the moment, and the conduct of his friends.

Gustav Droysen

THE STATESMAN OF "REALPOLITIK"

Gustav Droysen (1804–1884), a leading exponent of the "Prussian School" of history, was born in Prussia and studied at the University of Berlin, though he took no work with its greatest historian, Leopold von Ranke. His main interest as a student was in philology, yet despite his lack of historical training the brilliance of his first book, on Greek history, was sufficient to gain him a university appointment to teach history. He taught for a while at the University of Kiel, where, possibly because it was in the "border" area of Germany near Denmark, he became involved in the rising German nationalism of the time. He turned to modern history and incited his students to political activity, asserting that Germany's salvation depended on unity under Prussian leadership. Moving to a professorship at Berlin, he began his great work, a 14-volume History of Prussian Policy. Displaying vast scholarship, he suggested that Prussia was an independent entity, the heart of the German nation, and that through Prussia regeneration would come. An avowed Hegelian, he had a theory of organic growth in history which, together with a mystical concept of Germany's "mission," formed the theme of these volumes. Nor was his propaganda restricted to works of history. Droysen was a prolific pamphleteer and a leading proponent of the nationalist cause in 1848. His inclinations toward nationalism and "realpolitik" (that is, a politics of pragmatism and realism) can be sensed in the following selection from his two-volume biography of Gustavus Adolphus, published in 1870.

The opposition between Gustavus Adolphus and the House of Hapsburg derived from the attitude of both toward the question of supremacy in the Baltic. This was a purely political question.

Admittedly the Emperor had already begun to move in an outspokenly religious direction. He had concentrated at first on those territories in which he could act with the rights of a direct overlord, or where he could make the lofty authority of Imperial power effective. In his hereditary lands he had already begun the vigorous restoration of Papist teachings which had aroused the indignation of all Protestants. In the Imperial cities and small territories of central and southern Germany, he let the forced conversions take their course. But in his great Baltic project he took unmistakable care not to meddle with religious motives that would have created bitter enemies

From Gustav Droysen, *Gustav Adolf* (Leipzig, 1870), II: 3–5, 7, 24 and 26–28. Editor's translation.

among the thoroughly Protestant population of the north German plain, on whose cooperation he relied. . . .

From the beginning, the Emperor Ferdinand's Baltic policy was a subject requiring Gustavus Adolphus' constant observation and concern. It was his conviction that the House of Hapsburg aimed at the heart of the Swedish State. He expressed his convictions in many letters. The danger to the Protestant Church he did not once mention even in passing. Events in the Austrian hereditary lands, or in the southern part of the German Empire, lay on a distant horizon for Sweden. Gustavus was occupied with the danger that was closest at hand and which menaced him directly.

It is important to hold on to this point of view. This is the only way to find any unity or consistency in Gustavus Adolphus' policy. The history of Gustavus Adolphus . . . [up to the end of 1628] is filled throughout by the question of supremacy in the Baltic. This question brought him into conflict successively with Russia, Denmark and Poland. It entered a new stage when the House of Hapsburg, with its huge political network, took up this question and put its execution into Wallenstein's hands. At this point Gustavus Adolphus considered the frontiers of his kingdom endangered and menaced. They were not endangered by the hated Papist-Jesuit propaganda, but menaced by Hapsburg arms and ships. Now he was justified in stepping forward—not so much for oppressed Protestantism as for the threatened Fatherland.

As the Imperial arms advanced against Denmark and attacked Stralsund, it was Gustavus Adolphus' first thought to threaten Austria's flank from Poland. But the force of events carried him further. If Denmark were to be defeated, and Stralsund were to fall, then the Emperor would have won the foundation for supremacy in the Baltic. Gustavus Adolphus made alliances with Denmark and the city of Stralsund. He and Denmark helped the inhabitants of Stralsund. In Poland, the third theater of Baltic war, he himself fought the adherents of the Emperor.

Everything hung on the outcome in these three places. . . . Stralsund held out bravely, and Denmark retreated ignominiously from the fight. In the one place the opponents of the Hapsburgs won, and in the other the Emperor triumphed. Only in Poland did the struggle continue. . . .

The alliance with Stralsund was decisive for Swedish policy not only because it provided the King with his first secure base in Germany, but also just as much because it brought about a change in his plans against Austria.

For this daring, powerful and victorious Hanseatic city, with its hatred of Hapsburg arms, this "greatest port" in the Baltic, was a very different base for operations against Austria than hostile Poland, which would have had to be conquered or subdued before one used it as a jumping off point for an invasion of the Empire. . . . So Gustavus decided to bring the Polish business to an end, . . . [but his] wish to end the fight with Poland, so that he could move against the Emperor right away, was thwarted. . . . [Yet he was determined] not to be diverted from the war against the Emperor in the following year. He was convinced that the war . . . had to be carried into Germany so as to prevent the Emperor from coming toward Sweden. . . .

In September 1629 a six-year truce with Poland was finally reached . . . [and] now Gustavus Adolphus' hands were free. . . . He sent the Riksdag [Swedish national assembly] . . . a new "proposition" which started with the demand the Riksdag had expressed that he meet the danger and push the Papists out of the Baltic. . . . A thoroughly warlike spirit breathes through this document, which addressed itself to the representatives of the nation, calling them to rise above petty cares and concerns, to devote themselves completely to the holy cause of their Fatherland, to carry the nation along with him into the great war, and to bring him willingly their goods and their blood to sacrifice for their Fatherland. Here, where Gustavus goes over what is dear to them, what is endangered, what has to be protected from the menacing foe, here for the first time he mentions in terms of religion the great opposition, the dangers that Protestantism faced. In the wake of Imperial victories came the triumph of Catholicism. A conquered Sweden would have its faith destroyed. If one had to defend the Fatherland against this enemy, then one had to defend the faith. Gustavus Adolphus does not speak of a daring expedition, undertaken to protect the oppressed, to restore overthrown Protestantism in German lands. He does not think of the Edict of Restitution that had recently been imposed on Germany, nor of forcing the Emperor to rescind it by the strength of Swedish arms. The Fatherland, the freedom, power and faith of the Fatherland, these are the causes for which he calls his people to arms. . . .

Sweden is in danger from the House of Hapsburg, a danger that has to be met quickly and powerfully. One has to "defend the Father-land." The times are bad; the danger is great. . . . One is fighting for parents, wives and children, house and home—for the Father-land and the faith.

C. R. L. Fletcher
THE CHRISTIAN GENTLEMAN

C. R. L. Fletcher (1857–1934) taught history as a fellow of Magdalen College, Oxford, and then, after World War I, at Eton. An ardent Anglican Protestant, his beliefs were strongly apparent in all his writings. He was best known for two general works on English history. His five-volume Introductory History of England *was highly popular, as was the* School History of England *which he wrote in collaboration with Rudyard Kipling, the famous author. His biography of Gustavus Adolphus, from which the following selection is taken, was origi-nally published in 1890. Typical of the traditional idealization of the Swedish King, Fletcher's portrayal represents the very point of view that Droysen had been trying to undermine.*

The Thirty Years' War may be viewed from two aspects—an European and a German one. In respect of the first, it was the last of the great religious wars, closing the epoch of Reformation and Counter Refor-mation, proving to the Catholic powers of Europe that their ideal unity was no longer attainable, and teaching mankind, by the rudest possible process, the hard lesson of toleration. In respect of the second, it had a somewhat similar effect. Germany was an Europe in miniature; her nominal unity under the Hapsburgs was a parallel to the Catholic ideal unity of Europe under the Pope and the Emperor. This unity was blasted forever by the muskets of the opposing armies. But worse than this; when the war began Germany was a rich country, as the countries of Europe then went. She was really full of cities, which, though their main threads of commerce were fast snapping,

Reprinted by permission of G. P. Putnam's Sons from *Gustavus Adolphus* by C. R. L. Fletcher (London, 1890). The selections have been taken from the Capricorn paper-back edition (New York, 1963), pp. 51–52, 94–96 and 286–288.

might yet fairly be called very flourishing. When the war ended she was a desert. . . .

It is, however, from neither of these aspects that we have mainly to consider this disastrous war. We have to look at it from a third point of view—the Swedish. In this aspect Germany merely becomes the stage on which our Hero is to fret his brief hour, and to do the deeds for the good cause of Protestantism which have entitled him to the garland of immortality. . . .

Gustavus . . . [in 1629] seriously prepared for the German war. Was he right or wrong? Were his aims personal—for glory; or, national—for Sweden; or religious—for the faith? I can give no direct answer to such a question, nor can anyone. All human motives are mixed, and, if there is one lesson that history teaches, it is that no principle works in exclusion. But we must beware of judging Gustavus in the light of the later history of Sweden. That his countrymen did imbibe a taste for foreign conquest and foreign gold is undoubted, and it brought about the ruin of a noble country. But if his motives were as pure, as I believe them in the main to have been; if they were resistance to the tyranny of Austria, defense of his fatherland, and the rescue of Germany, we must pause before we lay at his door the later foreign ambition of his countrymen.

Another question irresistibly presents itself. What were his ultimate intentions? Did he—seeing, as he must have clearly seen, the corrupt condition of the German Empire, the absolute necessity of its reconstruction, dream of reconstructing it under a Protestant head? And was that head to be himself or someone else? I think the best answer to that question is found in the simple fact that his ideas developed as he went on. In December 1628, he wrote to Oxenstiern: "Here is a plan, from which you can gather at least the feasibility of my ideas. You say we haven't money to pay troops for more than four months; granted; but once let us plant our foothold sure" (he means on German soil), "and God and the hour will teach us how to strenghten ourselves further." It is the strong dash of knight-errantry combined with lofty aims that separates Gustavus Adolphus from his contemporaries. There were knights-errant in plenty (like Christian of Brunswick) in the field, but in Gustavus alone met the knight-errant, the statesman, and the king. That he wanted Pomerania as a bastion for the crown of Sweden is nothing whatever to the point.

He could not go to war for nothing. His wide and new relations on the Baltic made it imperatively necessary that future kings of Sweden should be princes of the Empire. . . .

It was not as a heathen Norseman that he . . . lived and died; rather as a Christian gentleman. If I were asked to find a parallel to him among those who have controlled the destinies of the world, I should pitch upon Saint Louis, King of France—in whom also were combined the three greatest qualities of a ruler of men, Justice, Courage, and Devotion. Saint Louis, born out of due time, lacked the fourth great quality whch was so rarely displayed in Gustavus, a quality or virtue which is indeed in itself but a daughter of Justice —Tolerance. The true glory of the King of Sweden was that he was the champion of Protestantism. Protestantism, though here and there it has been intolerant, and has used its triumphs unmercifully, has always led to Freedom, and Freedom to Toleration. And Toleration has been the great—the only really great—achievement of the Modern World. . . .

On June 21, 1634, the mortal remains of the Lion of the North were laid to rest in the Riddarholm church at Stockholm. There in a marble sarcophagus, under the tattered banners which tell of his earthly triumphs, lies the Hero of Sweden.

What was his character? . . . Simple, brave, passionate, truthful, devout; with the highest sense of his kingly dignity, and a yet higher sense of his great mission on earth, it is not unfair to say of him that he had a single eye to the work God had given him to do. More cannot be said of any man.

What were his aims? That has always been a great problem. But, if any one may be supposed to have known his mind, it surely was Axel Oxenstiern, with whom, during his whole reign, he lived upon terms of intimacy so affectionate to be very uncommon between great men of equal rank, but rare indeed between a subject and his sovereign. And all Oxenstiern's utterances on the subject have the same ring: "A great Scandinavian Empire, if you will. The Baltic and the Baltic coasts for Sweden. But NOT the crown of the Holy Roman Empire."

Swede and Vasa to the backbone, it was his own country after all that had most to bewail his loss. But the passionate grief in the streets of Stockholm found more than echo in every Protestant town in Europe—and in many Catholic; but most in that down-trodden Germany, to which he had appeared like a deliverer from on high, and which a Swedish historian finely calls his "dear Fosterland." For that land his death had almost as great an effect as his living deeds. It sanctified a cause which the German princes themselves had only known how to betray. He had been the first to set a bound to the tyranny which Germany was powerless to resist, and which would, if not resisted, have spread far beyond Germany, even far beyond distant Sweden. And for that reason Germany, Sweden, and mankind count him among their heroes.

Nils Ahnlund

THE CAUSE OF PROTESTANTISM AND FREEDOM OF CONSCIENCE

Nils Ahnlund (1899–1957) was born in Uppsala, Sweden, and became professor of history at the University of Stockholm in 1928. Ahnlund's doctoral thesis was on Gustavus Adolphus, and he published a number of important studies of Gustavus, Oxenstierna and early seventeenth century Sweden. His biography of Gustavus, Gustav Adolph the Great, originally published in 1932, is one of the most popular as well as scholarly accounts of the King's life. He also wrote on other periods of Swedish history. The English translation of his biography of Gustavus, from which extracts follow, was published in 1940.

How far Gustav Adolf is to be considered a "champion of the faith," and how far a "politician," is a question which in a strictly historical aspect misses the point. It was only natural that the safety and advantage of his country should shape his decision upon all occasions where it was a question of employing national means. Yet there was a firm inner core of religious motive within this demand for security. Like his father, but with more conscious purpose, Gustav Adolf strove to bring the interests of Sweden into harmony with the general inter-

From Nils Ahnlund, *Gustav Adolf the Great,* tr. M. Roberts (Princeton, 1940), pp. 267, 272–275 and 281–283. Copyright 1940 by the American-Scandinavian Foundation. Reprinted by permission.

ests of Protestantism. In one sense his policy was a policy of national interest, but at bottom it implied the consistent application of a philosophy of life to the problems of statesmanship. If this philosophy did not perhaps invariably act directly upon his policy, there was, nevertheless, always an indissoluble connection between the welfare of Sweden under the new dynasty, on the one hand, and the success or failure of the attempts to safeguard the Reformation throughout the world, on the other. As a modern Catholic historian testifies: "For Gustav Adolf there was an almost complete coincidence between his own interests and those of Protestantism." Such was his fundamental position; and naturally, with his ardent and sanguine temperament, he felt that his policy was Protestant through and through. . . .

"The evangelical cause" is a concept which appears again and again in the political negotiation of the time. It implies, without more precise definition, the obvious measure of common interest and common need as between Protestant states when face to face with the other great religious faction. "The common cause" (*causa communis*) is another name for the same idea. Gustav Adolf employed these and similar expressions more often than most of his contemporaries. He applied them in all good faith to his own aspirations and his own aims. This came the more easily to him because of his uncompromising enmity to Rome and his consequent need to find a practical link between Swedish policy and the general interests of Protestantism. If the Protestant cause, as the years went by, came ever more frequently to be termed "the cause of the oppressed and needy," Gustav Adolf . . . was well aware of the reasons that had produced this unhappy alteration. He was anxious, too, that the Lutheran people of Sweden should not for one moment be lulled into a false sense of security. . . .

As events followed hard on one another, they gave irrefutable confirmation to the king's idea of the dangerous situation of evangelical Christendom. The prescience of his judgment seemed borne out by the logic of the situation, as it gradually revealed itself. That danger was approaching, that it was close at hand—that was precisely what he had always told them. And it drew nearer and nearer, sweeping new regions into its scope, closer and ever closer to the frontiers of the country. "I today, thou tomorrow," as Gustav Adolf with an undertone of deep seriousness remarked in a letter of 1621 to Duke Adolf Friedrich of Mecklenburg. The allusion was to Friedrich of the Palatinate, whose unhappy fate many of the German Lutherans viewed with some indifference. In due time the duke of Mecklenburg shared his fate and his exile. At last the triumph of the emperor assumed the form of a real revolution. All Germany to the shores of the North Sea and the Baltic seemed delivered into his hand. "As one wave follows another, so the Catholic League batters at our gates."

It is unnecessary to recapitulate the well known events that marked Sweden's gradual intervention in the war. That fear of the growth of Imperial power in the Baltic played an enormous part in the decision is as undeniable as anything can well be; but that there was consequently implied any weakening or abandonment of the religious struggle as a motive for action, and as a reality of politics, can only be contended by those who are the victims of preconceived ideas. It was no accident that Gustav Adolf in a proposition to the Estates in 1627 should have spoken of "the Christian Church in the Baltic," or that he should have loved to speak of "the papists" in this connection. To contend that the well attested feeling which drove the nation into permanent hostility to the Roman Church was not subordinated to a purely secondary factor in a situation which the lessening of the distance between the two sides had suddenly exacerbated is to put a wholly false interpretation upon the history of the preceding decade. . . .

In 1637, in the course of a debate in the Rad,[1] we find Axel Oxenstierna declaring that the defense of religion was not the primary reason for the king's intervention in Germany. It is important to notice how the chancellor himself develops this remark in the sequel. The main reason, he says, was in fact that Sweden and her Protestant friends might rest secure and undisturbed in politics and church; it was a question not so much of religion as of *status publicus,* in which religion was itself included. Oxenstierna's contention is thus not that political reasons were predominant, independently of religious motives, but that the latter were bound up in the former, in other words that both motives operated in inextricable combination. Such a line of thought was entirely natural in that age. What the chancellor was

[1] The Assembly of the Swedish nobility.—Ed.

concerned to deny was the idea that religion was fought for as an end in itself, divorced from the welfare of the state and the interests of the country. The battle for the faith is indeed fought out with the weapons of the spirit, but the state is none the less bound to safeguard religion and protect it against threats and violence from within and without.

Gustav Adolf was a statesman of this way of thinking. To expect anything else of him would be to apply utopian standards to his work as the champion of Protestantism. With all his hardy enterprise he was still obliged to keep his aspirations within the limits of the attainable. His responsibilities to his country compelled him to it, however much his love of action and his imagination might drive him to extract the utmost from his opportunities. The program for a settlement with the emperor, which was kept ready from the autumn of 1626 onwards, might seem bold enough in view of the actual posture of affairs, but it was at least untainted by visionary extravagances. Gustav Adolf fixed his attention in the first place upon the restoration of the *status quo* in those parts of North Germany where it had been so violently disturbed—Upper and Lower Saxony—and in particular in the Baltic coastal region. . . .

And yet the Gustav Adolf who went over to Germany in 1630 will always seem more than a mere politician weighing risks before undertaking a gamble, and calculating chances in the moment of crisis. Axel Oxenstierna perceived the deeper, more inaccessible complexities of his character, when in a famous passage he spoke of the *impetus ingenii* which drove the king to action, and of the *dispositio divina* which he obeyed on such occasions. . . .

Was it for freedom of conscience that Gustav Adolf was fighting?

It is a question which has been answered negatively or with hesitation, even by those who in other respects give him a high place in history. The true answer seems to be that in the course of his struggle he attained at last a standpoint which may be said without misinterpretation to have been that of freedom of conscience.

When with the assent of his people he took up arms in an effort to stem the tide of events—for that was his real aim—he knew himself to be acting in his own defense. Purely political arguments contributed much to that decision; yet the protection of the evangelical faith was an integral part of his conception. Tolerance for such as differed from him—at any rate as far as Roman Catholicism was concerned—had never been part of his policy. By inheritance and from his own experience he felt himself to be its avowed foe and chief antagonist. Yet at the climax of his career his behavior presents a very different aspect.

The fact that he had now a Catholic power as his ally, in the shape of Richelieu's France, helped to cause this change. By the Treaty of Bärwalde [with France] he had engaged himself not to molest German Catholics in the exercise of their faith. The question seemed hardly at that time (January 1631) of burning importance. Nevertheless it is clear from the fact that Gustav Adolf had already decided to stand as a candidate for the electoral crown of Poland . . . that he had already made his choice and resolved on his attitude, irrespective of the doubtful chances of the German war. It was natural, no doubt, that he should look for support first to the relatively numerous Polish Dissidents; but the whole idea of his candidature, whether really seriously intended or no, must be taken as a recognition of the fact that he saw no reason why Protestants should not live peaceably side by side with the Catholics who formed the great majority of the inhabitants of Poland. To destroy Catholicism root and branch was in itself a scheme too foolhardy to win acceptance from such a political realist. From this point of view, therefore, he could with a clear conscience declare, to those Catholic powers who were enemies of the Hapsburgs, that he was not waging a religious war. To charge him with self-contradiction in this matter is to betray an imperfect understanding of his true purpose.

The nearer Gustav Adolf drew to Catholic Germany in its own home, the more bound he was to accept consequences which were logically inevitable. . . . Was then the recognition of the principle of toleration, to which he so often committed himself towards the close of his life, forced upon him by circumstances? If by "forced" we mean that he felt it to be cramping or hindering him, then the answer is No. Everything tends to show that it represented his sincere conviction, that it was part of a conscious philosophy. He felt convinced that it was the only policy for a statesman who aimed not only at destructive but at constructive action. For all his violent opposition to Rome in his earlier years, he had never been a religious fanatic. His moderate attitude towards Calvinism, and his view of the Greek Church, had already placed him among those who were able to rise above the narrow spirit of their age. And apart from all religious sympathies and antipathies, there was a dynamic element fundamental to his character which drove him in the same direction. When he considered that he had staked his honor he was not the man to be content with half-measures. . . . And finally—how was he to accomplish his work, the scope of which had so suddenly expanded, if he did not concern himself to establish a lasting peace between the religions of the Holy Roman Empire?

Thus in the end he threw away all reservations even in regard to Catholicism, and in language and action took a humane tolerance for his watchword. . . .

Michael Roberts
THE PRACTICAL STATESMAN

Michael Roberts, born in Lancashire in 1908, was educated at Oxford where he received his doctorate in 1935. He has taught at Oxford, in South Africa, and at present is professor of history at The Queen's University, Belfast. His main work has been in Swedish history, but he has also written on an early nineteenth century English political party and on modern South African history. He has published a number of articles and books on Sweden, as well as the translation of the book from which the Ahnlund selection was taken, but his two-volume history of Sweden during Gustavus' reign is his most important work. Published in the 1950s, it is a monumental piece of scholarship and as close to definitive as such a work can be. The following selections come from Volume 2, published in 1958.

The average Protestant abroad, knowing little of high politics, probably agreed with the Swedish trumpeter Theet, who knew very well (for the army padres had told him) that Gustav Adolf went over to Germany to defend the cause of true religion. Since that day, his-

From Michael Roberts, *Gustavus Adolphus: A History of Sweden, 1611–1632*, vol. 2 (London, 1958), pp. 418–421, 423–425 and 780–781. Reprinted by permission of Longmans, Green, and Co. Ltd.

torians have debated the matter at intervals; but they have not been much more successful than contemporaries in arriving at an agreed conclusion. Was it religion or politics, idealism or ambition, that drove him on?

To Gustav Adolf's contemporaries the question would have seemed improperly framed. It was not their habit to keep politics and religion in watertight compartments, either in action or in thought. If they laid greater emphasis for a moment on the one, they did not thereby exclude the other. It is easy to find statements which seem to put the whole venture upon a basis of political calculation: thus on 27 October 1629 Gustav Adolf stated flatly to the *råd* that the prime cause of war was imperial designs upon Sweden and the Baltic. Yet on 3 February 1633 Oxenstierna wrote to [the prominent Swedish nobleman] Salvius (whom it would have been quite purposeless to try to mislead) that the King's aim had been "first and foremost to liberate these and all his correligionists and relatives in the Empire from the popish yoke." The two statements were but different aspects of the same thing. Gustav Adolf was neither the Ideal Protestant Hero of nineteenth-century Swedish historiography nor the *Realpolitiker* of Droysen. He was compounded of both these elements, and hence different from either. . . . Religion was still a fundamental of life, and therefore of politics; it formed an essential element in the state's welfare, in the liberty and happiness of the individual. . . . Of all the national rights and liberties which might be threatened by developments south of the Baltic, none was more precious than that right of spiritual self-determination which had been the gain of the Reformation. It is futile to deny the importance of the religious motive in shaping Gustav Adolf's policy. . . . The whole course of his policy, from the early twenties onwards, demonstrated his concern for the evangelical cause, and his willingness to postpone his own more national quarrels to the claims of that cause—provided he were not asked to adventure Sweden's resources upon an obviously unsound bottom—was manifested more than once.

Nevertheless, it is clear that a policy based on a synthesis of this sort may be distorted, consciously or unconsciously, into a policy of political aggression, and religious conviction be harnessed to the daemon of a conqueror. . . . It has been suggested . . . that the King's object was really the creation of a great empire of Scandinavia;

and an observation once let fall by Oxenstierna is adduced as ground
for this view. . . . The evidence upon which it rests turns out upon
inspection to be imaginary. Oxenstierna never made the remark attributed to him: what he did say was that if Gustav Adolf had followed
his advice he might have become arbiter of the north—a very different matter. Nor is it necessary to attach too much importance to
the story, told to the *råd* at third hand in November 1635, that from
the beginning Gustav Adolf intended "an *imperium Macedonicum*" in
Germany, and a permanent diminution of the power of the Emperor.
There is not much more substance, either, in the contention that the
underlying motive in Swedish policy was economic. It has been
argued that Gustav Adolf's object was to establish a control of the
mouths of all the rivers flowing into the Baltic, and of all the main
ports upon that sea, in order to enrich himself by the levying of tolls,
as Kristian IV was enriching himself by the tolls at the Sound; or
that this was simply an extension of the old Swedish policy of trying
to control the trade between Muscovy and the West; or that the expedition to Germany was merely a means to obtain a vent for Swedish
copper, or to find capital resources for Usselincx's commercial enterprises. Now it is true that Gustav Adolf more than once alleged
imperial interference with Swedish trade and navigation as one of
his grievances against the Emperor; but in so far as this was seriously
meant, it was but another aspect of the purely political necessity for
the liberation of the Baltic coast from the threat of Hapsburg domination. If Gustav Adolf really put the control of the Russia trade high
among his list of objectives after 1617, it has left relatively little trace
in his intimate correspondence with Oxenstierna. It is, no doubt, quite
true that in the two years before 1630 the King had learnt the value
—the indispensability—of the Prussian tolls to the Swedish war bud-
get. It is also true that he adduced the prospect of imposing tolls on
the German rivers as one of the arguments in favor of intervention.
And there is no doubt . . . that he would have been glad to find a
vent for Swedish copper in Germany. But these were considerations
relatively new: the line of policy which led Gustav Adolf to Peene-
münde had begun to be apparent long before most of them were
heard of. Nor can this interpretation be squared with the King's
willingness to abstain from action in Germany if the Hapsburgs would
withdraw from the coastlands, and if the Germans themselves could

provide adequate security against their returning. The economic advantages which he undoubtedly sought in Germany were not ends in themselves: they were means to other ends—ends religious, ends political—and a recognition of the importance of economic factors does little to advance the enquiry into the nature of his real designs. . . .

It is true that there are indications that for some years before 1630 Gustav Adolf was contemplating more or less permanent annexations on the southern shore of the Baltic. . . . Yet in regard to each of them other explanations are possible. . . . On the eve of the invasion he had no great hope of a general settlement for Germany as a whole upon the basis of a return to 1618, still less a plan of his own for territorial or constitutional alterations within the Empire. And in so far as he hoped at this time for compensations for the injuries he had received, or indemnification for his war expenses—for *satisfactio*, as it was later to be termed—his ideas did not as yet take the form of territorial annexations.

Since the end of 1628 Gustav Adolf had from time to time put out statements of his grievances against the Emperor. The document known as *Appellatio ad Caesarem*, the letters to the Protestant Electors, the manifesto to the Regensburg meeting, were widely disseminated throughout Europe, and were obviously designed to influence public opinion. In part they were mere propaganda; and complaints of different kinds and varying weight were heaped up without much regard to logic or consistency, in order that the total effect might be as massive as possible. But the purpose of these documents was not only to justify Swedish policy to the world. They were meant also to justify it to Gustav Adolf himself. As an attentive reader of Grotius,[1] he knew well what latitude was permitted to him who waged a "just" war; and it was essential to prove that this war fell into that category. Grotius had laid it down that danger imminent and certain alone could justify the violation of neutrality; and since that was what Gustav Adolf had it in contemplation to do, there must be no doubt about the danger. On broad grounds he might feel convinced that he was justified; but there were times when he wondered whether his arguments would seem equally cogent to others. If he took and kept

[1] Hugo Grotius was the leading theorist of international law during this period.—Ed.

Wismar, for instance, would it not be "iniquitous" thus to deprive the Dukes of Mecklenburg of one of their towns? If he hung on to Stralsund after the imperialist threat had gone, would not that be a breach of treaty obligations? Would it not seem as though he had gone to Germany for no other purpose but to "amplify his realm"? It was not enough for him to feel that he had been in the right; he must be reassured that the public thought so too. As late as December 1630 he could address to the *rad* a long interrogatory, in which he rehearsed once more the familiar story of his injuries at the Emperor's hands, and appealed to them for an opinion as to whether they did not constitute a justification for his actions from the standpoint of international law. Gustav Adolf, indeed, had too tender a conscience to be a wholly convincing Goth.

Certainly he believed that the war which was beginning was essentially defensive in character: a war for the safety of Sweden, and equally a war to save the surviving remnant of German Protestantism. And he was above all concerned to ensure that he should not have this work to do twice over. He had at this moment no ally save Stralsund; he was beset by doubts and uncertainties; he was utterly unable to foresee the progress of events in Germany after he should have landed. He was, in short, in no position to hatch, nor was the *råd* likely to have endorsed, a grandiose scheme of conquest. Beyond the most general and vague notions, he cannot have had much idea what he should do when once the German campaign should have begun. He was going to Germany, not with any wild idea of overturning the constitution of the Empire, or of placing himself in the room of Caesar, nor even (on a more modest scale) of reconstituting the old Protestant Union under Swedish patronage; but with the intention of pushing Wallenstein's troops away from the coast, and somehow contriving that they should not come back. How that was to be done, he did not precisely know: perhaps by a shorter or longer Swedish occupation of the endangered areas, perhaps by a system of alliances; but first, and most essential of all, by military power. The indispensable prerequisite to any stable settlement was the eviction of the imperial armies from the coastlands and the infliction upon them of defeats severe enough to deprive them of the power of further mischief. No political system was likely to be worth the building until a real victory was won: the aim of diplomacy, for as far ahead as he or Oxenstierna could see, must be to obtain military cooperation, military alliances, military security. The immediate object was limited to north Germany. As to whether north Germany could be esteemed safe so long as the south was in bondage, he did not at this stage enquire too closely. The search for security would later take him into paths he certainly had not yet dreamed of, would commit him to ventures which in May 1630 he would probably have rejected out of hand as chimerical; but these thorns were as yet concealed. As his newly landed soldiers fell to digging themselves in under the eye of their commander, the prospects, though hazardous, did not seem too complex, nor the immediate goal impossibly distant. The methods to be employed to reach it might still be uncertain; but the goal itself stood clear. It was never to be quite as clear again.

*   *   *

Gustav Adolf was essentially an empirical statesman. He had no grandiose or cut-and-dried political plans. He dealt with situations as they arose, by successive expedients; or he prepared precautionary measures against menaces plainly impending. Some broad general aims he had: the security of his dynasty, the security of his country, the security of the Protestant religion; but on the whole his policy was the reaction to external pressures, and he himself would have considered it essentially defensive. Providence had not endowed him with a special gift of political divination, though he had, perhaps, a sufficiency of ordinary foresight. Security proved, as it has proved so often, a will o' the wisp, and the terms accepted by Sweden at Westphalia suggest that Gustav Adolf followed it too far. But security, not empire-building, was his real purpose; and he could not be expected to foresee that the territorial gains incidental to its pursuit might themselves one day be a source of weakness and danger. . . .

Gustav Adolf was the greatest of Swedish kings. Contemporaries were not sparing of their tributes; and by the generation that followed him he was called "The Great" as a matter of course. His military exploits; his salvation of German Protestantism; his death, which the pious might esteem but one remove from martyrdom; combined to throw a radiance upon the monarchy, clothing it with a prestige which it had never before enjoyed, associating it unforgettably with the martial glories of the nation. But Breitenfeld was not merely a national, it was also a religious triumph: in its appeal comparable less to Agincourt than to the Boyne. Church and crown, after a century of relations at best uneasy, at worst openly hostile, sealed their union in the blood of the slaughtered *tercios* [divisions] of the League. And the figure of the victor of that field was henceforward fixed unshakably, as no other Swedish king's, in the memories of all patriots. If today it is the portrait of Gustav Vasa—the founder of the realm, the wise economist on the throne—that stands on the Swedish banknotes, the image of Gustav Adolf lives as a national symbol in the popular consciousness. And every year still, in the murky slip-slop of a Stockholm November, the damp uniforms and dripping standards of the ceremonial parades evoke, with infinite melancholy, the fatal mists of Lützen. "King Karl the youthful hero"[2] is still—and will probably continue to be—an apple of discord among historians, a controversial figure fiercely fought over, a symbol around whom battle the champions of divergent outlooks on both past and present. But the voices raised against Gustav Adolf have been both few and feeble; and even the reaction against that school of historians which was antiaristocratic and promonarchical has left his reputation virtually undisturbed.

[2] King Charles XII of Sweden, who ruled from 1697 to 1718, and lost most of the territories that formed the Swedish Empire in a series of wars.—Ed.

Albrecht von Wallenstein

Albrecht von Wallenstein
MOTIVATION AND AIMS

Virtually everyone who has written about Albrecht von Wallenstein (1583–1634) has compared him to a meteor. The career of the minor landowner's son who married a rich widow, made a fortune in land speculation, achieved European-wide fame by providing the Emperor with an army and changing the destiny of Germany, and who then suffered a shattering collapse as the German princes and finally the Emperor turned against him, is the stuff of which legends are made. Perhaps only Napoleon in European history has been a more spectacularly successful self-made man, climbing to dizzy heights only to fall headlong into total disaster. But Wallenstein has exerted a particular fascination because historians have never been able to determine what his aims were. Unlike Gustavus, he clearly had no religious motivation— his army contained men of all faiths, and he spoke of crusades only against the Turks. But was he really a devoted servant of the Emperor, or only out for his own gain? Or, more idealistic than either of these, was he a man of peace who wanted primarily to bring the fighting to an end? No conclusive answers to these questions will ever be possible, because the evidence is contradictory and incomplete. Examples of the documents that are used to justify a favorable view are the following letters, in which Wallenstein states noble aims. The more cynical can look not to his letters—where the evidence, perhaps purposely, is nonexistent—but to his actions, notably his secret negotiations with the Emperor's enemies, Sweden and Saxony, in his last years. Each paragraph in the first section that follows comes from different letters he wrote in April 1629; the second section is taken from a letter of 23 October 1633. All the letters are taken from the monumental series of publications of Hermann Hallwich, a German historian who devoted his life to editing all the records of Wallenstein's career.

I

I have just discussed the war in Hungary at length with Count Tilly, and eventually I brought up the proposal that we go to war against the Turks. He jumped at the idea, embraced it wholeheartedly, and said that this would be a holy, glorious, easy, and necessary enter-

From Hermann Hallwich, ed., *Fünf Bücher Geschichte Wallensteins* (Leipzig, 1910), 2: 583–584; and *Briefe und Akten zur Geschichte Wallensteins (1630–1634)* (Vienna, 1912: Vol. 66 of Österreichische Geschichts-Quellen), 4: 397–398. Editor's translation.

prise. I told him that we had hoped to make preparations last year—and he approves of the idea. . . . If only there were peace in Italy [a reference to the Mantuan war], we could begin even this year to make moves toward Macedonia and Albania [in the Balkans].

Smashing the Turks would please me to the root of my soul, as it would Count Tilly, who told me, during a general discussion we were having, that there would be nothing more difficult in such an undertaking than finding a just cause for declaring war. For the rest, Count Tilly agrees with me completely that we ought to attempt such an advance exactly along the lines we worked out a number of years ago.

It would be better to turn our arms against the Turks [than use them in Mantua]. With God's help our Emperor would be able to place the Crown of Constantinople on his head within three years.

II

Yesterday Duke Franz Albrecht [Wallenstein's go-between in his negotiations with the Saxons] . . . urged me . . . to resume the negotiations, which had failed earlier only because of misunderstandings. I answered that now, as always, His Majesty's intention is to establish peace and unity in the Empire, and therefore I am commanded to seek the same ends. . . . Hence I want to pursue my campaign for the good of the Empire together with the Electors [of Saxony and Brandenburg], for we would soon be able to rid our land of all belligerents. They wanted me to get down to details, . . . but I made no response, because I do not want to get into specific negotiations—first Your Majesty [the Emperor] must prepare the way with the Electors. It is worth remembering, above all, that it would not be a bad thing to rid Your Majesty's lands not only of your enemies' forces but of all belligerents, and that in addition such a joint operation would mean, first, that the Electors' arms would be united with imperial arms, and second, that the College of Electors in general would be starting to join and support Your Majesty.

FIGURE 4. *Wallenstein,* a portrait by Van Dyck. Not only in his titles, but in his portraits as well, Wallenstein at the height of his fame demanded the treatment reserved for the greatest princes of Europe. He commissioned the most famous portraitist of the time to paint him in armor, holding the staff that symbolized earthly power. (*Bayerische Staatsgemäldesammlungen, München*)

Leopold von Ranke

THE EGOISTIC BUT IDEALISTIC
SEEKER OF PEACE

*Leopold von Ranke (1795–1886) was one of the founders of the modern study
of history. Born in Thuringia, he studied at Halle and Berlin and taught in a
school in Frankfurt on the Oder. From 1825 to 1872 he was professor of
history at the University of Berlin, where in 1833 he founded a famous seminar
which not only trained a generation of distinguished historians, but also
served as a model for much of the subsequent teaching of postgraduate history. During a research trip from 1828 to 1831 Ranke made the first extensive
investigations of the political and diplomatic documents in archives in Vienna,
Venice, Rome, and Florence. Although he was immensely prolific (his collected works fill 54 volumes), his books were always closely and carefully
based on the manuscript sources. His first work, a* History of the Latin and
Teutonic Peoples, 1494–1535, *was published in 1824 and immediately established his reputation. Its famous introduction suggested that the historian
merely had to describe the past as it actually was (a passing remark which
has been given much weighty significance, but which in context is no more
than a modest disclaimer in face of historians who attempt great judgments
in history). The books that followed ranged over many periods, but Ranke had
a particular interest in the sixteenth and seventeeth centuries. Not only his
first book, but histories of France, England, Germany, the Ottoman and
Spanish Empires, and the Popes were devoted to these centuries. His biography of Wallenstein, published in 1869, was the first serious attempt at an
impartial assessment of the most controversial figure in seventeenth century
German history. The hallmarks of Ranke's approach are apparent even in the
few short extracts from the biography that follow. His careful, modest,
scholarly evaluation broke completely from a tradition in which Wallenstein
had been either hysterically reviled or uncritically idealized (see Introduction).
Even recent analyses, despite the uncovering of new documents, have rarely
achieved the level of unemotional and convincing objectivity attained by
Ranke.*

If it is ever possible to assess the intentions of a prominent man when
he never put them into writing (and even if he had, they still might
not be entirely acceptable), using for evidence only his public pronouncements, his previous actions, and his current situation—and
uncertain areas in the depths of human endeavors and ambitions

From Leopold von Ranke, *Geschichte Wallensteins*, Vol. 23 of *Sämmtliche Werke*, 3rd
ed. (Leipzig, 1872), pp. 289–296, 298–300, 311, 313 and 317. Editor's translation.

will always remain—then I will venture to indicate the following as Wallenstein's principal aims [in his last years]. He hoped, with the help of the two north German Electors [Brandenburg and Saxony], to settle the situation in the Empire on the basis of religious freedom. This could not have been accomplished without doing justice to the Bohemian émigrés and to the Austrian hereditary lands in general, by a complete restoration of the constitution of the Estates. At the same time he wanted to satisfy the demands of the army, and also to establish the boundaries of his own territories and the future of his House. . . .

He was determined not to have his command taken away from him again. To prevent this happening, he concluded an agreement with the army: he made their aims his own and they solemnly promised in return that they would uphold his authority.

These were the main provisions of the agreement reached in Pilsen [a small Bohemian town about 50 miles southwest of Prague], but there were others. It was also decided that they would participate in the establishment of the peace that Wallenstein and the [two northern] Electors were planning. What would happen, however, if the Imperial court were to take the opposing view: if his peace were to be rejected and his dismissal from the generalship announced? . . . Wallenstein had been made a General by the Emperor, in whose name the army had been raised. If a split appeared, should not the service of the Emperor supersede obedience to the General? The ground on which Wallenstein stood, or on which he had placed himself, was already undermined. If he based his agreements with the army primarily on cash transactions, then Spanish subsidies were ready to satisfy demands which had so great an importance.

Events moved rapidly toward the moment of decision. . . .

On February 18 [1634] . . . a . . . decree was issued, and with it an order to the army, in which it was taken as proved that the Duke of Friedland [Wallenstein] had entered into a conspiracy to deprive the Emperor of his hereditary lands, his crown and his scepter, and to take them for himself. As Emperor and commander in chief, Ferdinand II directed the leading officers no longer to obey the ex-commander and his adherents. . . .

Could now the aura of the General balance the force of Imperial authority?

The first showdown was to be in Prague. And here, as elsewhere, the fate of most of the country hung on the decision in the capital. Wallenstein relied on the garrison, or rather . . . he did not doubt that they would obey his orders. However, the senior Colonel of the troops garrisoned in Prague, a man named Beck, had often spoken of the difference between the obedience he owed his General and the loyalty he owed his Emperor. On February 21 Wallenstein once more asked him for a declaration of allegiance. But Beck had already authorized his chief Lieutenant, as he set out for Pilsen, not to obey any of the commands that he might receive. . . .

This was the situation when Trčka [Wallenstein's brother-in-law and loyal supporter] prepared to inspect the route the Duke of Friedland wanted to take to Prague. The officer riding towards him, however, told him the unexpected news of what had just happened in the capital city.

The news was received in Pilsen while they were still putting into effect the agreements [with the army] reached a few days before. At first it seemed to be just an arbitrary action by the chief Lieutenant, which would be put right by a counter-order from the Colonel. But they soon realized how matters stood. The defection of Prague was also decisive because they had expected to bring together all of the army in the area, and then proceed to the great negotiations [for peace]. . . .

Trčka displayed wild, unruly impatience; [but two other loyal friends] Ilow [the Imperial Quarter-master] and Kinský [a leading Bohemian exile] . . . realized the importance of what had happened. Wallenstein above all understood the implications. Knowing that the peace negotiations could not have been further from their goal, he dismissed the Imperial adviser who had come to take part in the discussions. "I had peace in my hand," he told Colonel Beck, whom he saw only once more; but perhaps he still did not despair; after a moment of silence he added, "God is righteous." . . .

He understood the designs of his opponents in general, but he was never able to see through them or evaluate them in individual instances, or they would not have defeated him so easily. He always lived in the midst of his grand designs, in which nevertheless the public interest was mixed up with his private aims, though, if we do not misunderstand him, the former predominated. And it was all clothed in a self-confidence that blinded even Wallenstein himself. We must only regret that he did not keep his designs free of all false trimmings, and pursue them with greater circumspection and refinement. In his relations with his generals Wallenstein took into consideration only how much gratitude they personally owed him, and not that they might have some motive, given their position and some other circumstance, to turn against him. He relied much too much on those ties . . . which never really bound his generals and yet still offended the Emperor. The decrees not to obey his orders came as a surprise both to himself and to his friends. . . .

He now expected to conclude, in Eger [a small town on the Bohemian border almost 100 miles due west of Prague], an alliance with Arnim [the commander of Saxony's army]. Arnim was already on his way, and Wallenstein had made a definite arrangement with the Elector [of Saxony] about the alliance. The Duke expected to greet Arnim in the midst of his officers, put the finishing touches to the agreement that had been prepared, and then lay it before the Emperor. If [Ferdinand] refused it, he would take the path of force in alliance with Saxony, with whom he had already come to terms, and with Sweden, with whom he hoped to reach an understanding.

At the time everything seemed possible.

Among the pronouncements of Wallenstein during these days, related by trustworthy witnesses, were two which deserve particular notice. The first was that one had to show the world that it was possible to have an Emperor who was not of the House of Austria, which allowed itself to be ruled by Spaniards. The other referred to his personal position: if the Emperor no longer wanted to recognize him as his general, then he, too, did not want to have the Emperor as his commander. He could easily attach himself to another prince, but he would not let anyone be his commander again. He wanted to be his own commander and he had the resources to maintain himself as such.

The most pressing question for him was not whether he would inherit the Palatinate, or perhaps the crown of Bohemia. His experiences had aroused his ambition to break free of all subordination, and to assume an independent position among the leaders of the world. . . . If it became impossible to achieve this with the approval of the Emperor, then it would happen anyway with himself and the House of Austria on opposite sides.

This was not his original line of thought, but he was led to it by the force of circumstances. . . .

What projects he could have accomplished! He could have been King of Denmark, or overthrown the Turkish Empire, or once again after a hundred years have descended on Rome with German troops. In Germany he could have shattered the power of the Electors and the princes, and in fact the whole hierarchic system. All this could have been done in the service not only of the Emperor and the House of Austria, but also of his own ever-rising greatness and power. After his return to service he still hoped to achieve these aims, as well as peace in the Empire on the basis of equal rights for both faiths, with the approval of the Emperor. And nothing could have been more important for the future of the German nation than the success of this plan. . . . He now threw all of his highly personal, yet also idealistic, ambition into these aims. He did so with that exaggerated self-confidence, contemptuous of all else, based on the supposed favor of the stars, that was his alone. He expected to overcome the difficulties growing for him at court by taking a firm stand at the head of the army. . . . When now the supreme command of the army was taken away from him . . . he decided to free himself completely from the power of the House of Austria. He had envisioned an eventual alliance with their opponents, even with France. Should he now perhaps have come forward in the name of this power, as some of his supporters suggested? Nothing had been prepared for it, and it would have put him in a false position with regard to the German Empire. He had enough courage to try to establish an independent power around which the opponents of the House of Austria could unite so as to overthrow [the Hapsburgs] in Germany and Italy.

This plan undoubtedly contradicted his own background. For he had advanced primarily because of the dynastic interest [of the Hapsburgs]. . . . He had established himself as their most powerful supporter in their hereditary lands and had attacked the privileges of the Estates which he now wanted to bring to life again. Everything that he had done and accomplished up to that time rested on the authority of the Emperor. The Imperial name still commanded universal respect.

Those who tried to undermine the hereditary powers on whom Europe's kingdoms and social structure were based were still reviled and themselves destroyed. Could [Wallenstein] succeed in such an enterprise? . . .

As Oxenstierna said, Wallenstein started more than he could finish. As soon as [the Hapsburgs] turned against him, he was bound to succumb to Imperial power and the might of the House of Austria. . . .

Wallenstein, who first tried most determinedly [to make the Emperor change his policy] . . . and then only feebly tried [to join the Emperor's enemies, failed because] he had to fight born princes, whose authority had been firmly established for centuries and was united to all other national institutions. . . .

When Wallenstein was murdered at Eger in February 1634, there arose at the court in Vienna itself two opposing views of his guilt. The first ran as follows. He had embarked on a highly treasonous conspiracy to chase the Emperor out of Vienna and to destroy the House of Austria in Germany and even in Spain. It enlarged on the way he then intended to reorganize the European state system. The other view denied all this. It noted that if Wallenstein had intended to do the Emperor harm, he could have done so long before without any trouble. Now, however, quite different resources and people than those at his disposal were needed for such a purpose. Besides, was it conceivable that a man plagued by illness, whose life, according to the doctors, could not have lasted another two years, a man who had no heirs, could have wanted to set one of his Emperor's crowns on his own head and then fight for it?

The crime of which he has been accused will never be proved. After he and his close associates were murdered, their papers were seized, but nothing conclusive could have been found. For if it had, the investigation would have been brought to a speedy and decisive conclusion.

Josef Pekař

THE COWARDLY AND MEGALOMANIC TRAITOR

What have we found? A weakling crushed by physical afflictions, confused by superstitions, impelled by titanic and megalomanic schemes of revenge, a cowardly traitor, and a foolish intriguer.

We cannot honestly say that we completely understand this character, that we know the secret and dark recesses of his soul. For fleeting moments he strikes a chord in us which threatens to destroy many a carefully researched conclusion. It overwhelms us and fills us with doubt. This violent and passionate, pitiless and insatiable man, who terrorized his contemporaries with imprecations and terrible curses—this same man stretched his hands eagerly toward heavenly secrets, listened longingly to the mystic language of the stars, and was time and again thrown into fits of "wrathful melancholy." The incompleteness of the sources permits us only rarely to have such an insight into the depths of his secret vision—when it is possible, however, then its effect is all the more powerful. We need only pick the passage from the inquest where General Scherffenberg testified about his audience with the Duke [Wallenstein] in January 1634. The General was summoned to the Duke. When he announced himself, he received no reply. A long silence followed—then suddenly Wallenstein half rose out of the bed in which he was resting and called out: "O peace! O peace! O peace!" Or we can recall a scene on that terrible February morning when Trčka brought the news that the majority of the army supported the Emperor, and that there was nothing to do but flee to Eger. The Duke called Colonel Beck and after a long silence said: "Now I had peace in my hand . . . God is righteous. . . ."

Is this not a sorrowful resignation in face of the collapse of a high and noble endeavor? Is it not the pious exclamation of an afflicted,

From Josef Pekař, *Wallenstein 1630–1634, Tragödie einer Verschwörung* (Berlin, 1937), I: 692–696, 698–699, 701–702, 704–705, and 708–709. Copyright 1937 by Alfred Metzner Verlag, Berlin. All rights, particularly the rights of translation, are reserved. Reprinted by permission of the publisher. For information on the author and on editions of this work, see page 80. Editor's translation.

struggling soul? Does all this not remind one of Schiller's idealistic Wallenstein? And now let us compare this picture with the Wallenstein whom we have come to know from many other witnesses, from his own words and deeds, from his entire behavior! Perhaps the coarseness of his times and occupation, the harsh race for success, and the rigor of his situation did not blot out all traces of the tender spirit that was battling against temptation. Perhaps in this dichotomy, in this internal dissension, lies the explanation of his hesitations, his doubts, his confusions and retreats, and the deficiencies in his capacity for resolute action. We shall have to be satisfied with this "perhaps"—the paucity and incompleteness of the sources permit us no sure answer. They do not give us the right to probe sceptically into the obscure shadows of his spirit, to close our eyes to any reflection of a nobler character that may shine through.

"I had peace in my hand!" said the Duke to Colonel Beck. "Nothing will come of the peace," he had said to Trčka on September 14. "I have no more burning desire than to found a lasting peace in the Empire,"—he wrote and told Arnim time and again. "The armies themselves will make peace, and the Emperor will not be able to interfere," he repeated to Bubna in May 1633. Was this only a great plea for peace, a striving for the peace that millions longed for, a high and unselfish goal? . . . We have mentioned that no trace of this longing for peace can be found either in the negotiations of 1631 with Gustavus Adolphus, or in Kinský's disclosures in Dresden in the spring of 1633, or in the plans of August 1633, or in the dealings with Feuquières [the French ambassador] and Oxenstierna in 1634. We have also shown that all the other peace proposals could have been implemented only by a rebellion against the Emperor, and that the Duke spoke of peace because he wanted a war with the Emperor. . . . "He always used the pretext of peace," Duke Franz Albrecht later said of Wallenstein when he was asked whether Wallenstein would have wanted to become King of Bohemia—and in this explanation lies . . . the single and only truth. Wallenstein sheltered his designs behind a facade of peace because he needed slogans and ideas in whose name he could fight out his personal battle with the Emperor and his allies. In this tremendous European battleground, where leaders on both sides could transform their supporters' adherence to real or imagined goals into fanaticism, where people really fought for their beliefs, for freedom of conscience, and for the freedom of their Fatherland, Wallenstein could not propose a program of naked revenge and ambition. He did not dare put himself up as a symbol for his armies and allies. And so he entered the arena of the German Empire, where France pretended to be struggling for liberation from tyranny, and where Sweden feigned or at least artificially increased an enthusiasm for freedom of conscience, with the sympathetic slogan of lawful peace. It is significant that nobody ever believed him. Arnim . . . knew that Wallenstein worked for "the enlargement of his possessions and raising of his status," and the French and Swedes were also not deceived. In the summer of 1633 a large part of the Empire was full of the news about the impending revolt of the Friedländer [Wallenstein] against the Emperor, but not once do we encounter the suggestion that the Duke wanted peace. . . .

Peace negotiations were the best way to mask the secret discussions whose result was supposed to have been a new outbreak of war in its most dangerous form—in the shape of a revolt by the Imperial army against the Emperor, with the help of the enemy army they were supposed to overcome!

Wallenstein could have approached the situation in one of two ways. We can call the first the German, and the second the Bohemian. The first was recommended by Hans Georg von Arnim, who guided Saxony's policy. The malcontents within the Empire who were hostile to the Hapsburgs and conspired with Wallenstein wanted the second, as did the Bohemian émigrés, Sweden and France. According to the first plan, the Duke should have been satisfied with the enforcement of a just peace that would have restored the religious and political situation as it had existed in the Empire (and hence also in Bohemia) before the war. As far as possible, this peace would have freed Germany from the influences and armies of foreign nations—Swedes, Frenchmen and Spaniards. If the occasion arose, it would have been enforced even against the Emperor by the combined armies of Wallenstein, Saxony and Brandenburg. The second plan envisioned the destruction of the power of the House of Austria all the way down the line with the direct help of the Swedes and the French. It aimed at the secession of Bohemia from Hapsburg territories and the election of a new King for Bohemia. If Arnim strongly urged the first proposal, he did so primarily to keep the Duke from the second path; the second was pressed by Wallenstein's close friends Trčka and Kinský as well as by their émigré friends. This second plan fulfilled completely, perhaps uniquely, Wallenstein's need for power and revenge; this way the Duke of Bavaria would get his just deserts, and this way there beckoned the glittering reward of the crown of Bohemia. . . . To Wallenstein's way of thinking, these two plans were incompatible and struggled for supremacy. The acceptance of the generalship forced him to go back from plans of open revolt to the more circumspect and better concealed first project (at the negotiations with Arnim in 1632). Then in 1633 the Duke at first pursued both plans separately so as to bring them boldly together shortly thereafter—in August 1633. And finally, after a return to the first plan at the end of September and in October 1633, he sought in the last two months of his life to accomplish both possibilities at the same time. . . .

Wallenstein had neither the essential strength of character nor the necessary courage for carefully wrought conspiracies. . . . He was not the kind of hero who gambled everything on one play and defied fate with resolute action. Only in his big words, in his outbreaks of cursing, when he and his army were going to chase the Emperor out of his lands and into Spain, when he swore the destruction of the Duke of Bavaria and other enemies, or when he assigned the kingdoms and dukedoms of half Europe to new rulers, then he seemed a hero. But in fact he was a calculating man who wanted to act only when he was certain. Because of all his precautions and waiting for more favorable circumstances he was never capable of any action at all. A careful speculator, who wanted to destroy the power of the House of Austria in Europe, he still thought it unfriendly, when he noticed that Vienna did not trust him, to be asked to prove his loyalty to the Emperor. . . . He let enemies promise him the Bohemian crown while he was demanding in Vienna the enlargement of his Dukedom of Friedland into neighboring territories, so that no possible advantage would be missed on any side. A blatant intriguer, he agreed to unite his regiments with his enemies while at the same time . . . he sent assurances to Vienna that he had no secret designs against the Emperor or religion. . . . He behaved stupidly in every direction, and his stupidity brought about his catastrophe. . . .

The literature on Wallenstein . . . has overlooked the fact that Wallenstein was by birth a Bohemian and a member of the Bohemian gentry, that his leading friends and associates in the struggle against the Emperor were Bohemians, and that in the territories of the Bohemian crown—this most important power within the borders of the German Empire—there had been building up for decades a religious and political situation out of which the plan for a rebellion by the opponents of the Hapsburgs could emerge quite naturally and logically. . . . Yet even in the "Bohemian" part of his program, which after all was closely connected through its Protestant overtones with the "German" part, we must not look for idealistic motivation such as Bohemian patriotism in the sense of traditional dissatisfaction with the House of Austria. All the same, the Duke must have felt closer to these sentiments than to any of German origin, because he was deeply involved in the fate and land of Bohemia by ties of tradition, extraction, residence, language and friendship. . . .

Wallenstein was a product of a part of Bohemian society whose condition at that time was symptomatic of the corruption and decay in the body of the nation. . . . The unbridled struggle for power, riches and glory, which can be seen as an echo of the spirit of the Renaissance in our land, found in him its greatest exponent. While growing up before the war Wallenstein had already absorbed the spirit of this struggle, and he became its most distinguished representative when he revelled victoriously in the booty of the conquered kingdom after the battle of the White Mountain. . . . Wallenstein forcibly reminds one of the predatory Italian condottiere. He also belongs to the Renaissance in his aspirations toward the grandiose. . . . But the vehemence of his disposition, with its astonishing contrasts of light and dark, and his confident investigation of the promises and warnings of the stars, place him fully in his Baroque surroundings. This urgency to plan and justify his actions with heavenly approval fatefully darkened the clarity of his aims, and possibly was the main reason for his ultimate failure. Even as a son and adherent of the Czech national community he aspired to be independent, to free himself from traditional ties to his Fatherland and achieve a higher status. . . . Already in the year 1609, when he had Kepler cast his horoscope, he asked if it were true that his Bohemian compatriots would be his greatest enemies. This, too, demonstrates the unnaturalness of his likes and dislikes. Italians and Spaniards betrayed him, Germans for the most part abandoned him, but the "doltish Bohemian Johnny" knew how to die with him! . . .

When Ranke wrote that Wallenstein's conspiracy would have forfeited the right to fascinate posterity if it had been nothing more than the product of its originator's egoism, . . . we know that Ranke had in mind the goal of German patriotism, the freeing and liberation of the Empire. . . . The German historian missed the principal and undoubted significance of Wallenstein's tragedy, a significance that has its roots in the connection with the hopes of the Bohemian émigrés. . . . It is clear that Wallenstein's plans included the political demands of a leader of the émigrés, and that on the triumph or collapse of his plans depended the dreams, aspirations and hopes of the humiliated elements of the whole nation. In this way the Friedländer's conspiracy became a part of national history, a natural phase in its development, a particularly exciting epoch which captures our attention more easily than any other because of the greatness of its hopes and the pain of the disappointment. Whatever we may think about the causes of the Bohemian revolt, we cannot help being deeply moved by this émigré community which, in the midst of a whirlpool of deceptive parties, slogans and programs, fought and struggled honestly and devotedly for its beliefs and its Fatherland. After fruitless expectations and many years of disappointment, Wallenstein seemed to be a man capable of guiding all their endeavors to a great victory. . . . Instead of the triumph came the catastrophe. It is this long drawn out death struggle . . . that makes the powerful impression in this story. Behind the personal drama of the man from Friedland there rises up, growing in the distance, an overpowering drama, the tragedy of a shattered nation, whose last cry also rang out in the citadel of Eger.

Heinrich Ritter von Srbik
THE TORTURED IDEALIST

Heinrich Ritter von Srbik (1878–1951) was born in Vienna, where he studied at the university and then taught history. He was professor of history at the University of Graz from 1912 to 1922 before returning to the University of Vienna, where he remained as professor until 1945. Always deeply involved in Austrian history, he refused many invitations to teach at German universities. His books covered many periods, and included both general works, often dealing with the relation of Austrian to German history, and detailed studies such as a history of Austro-Hungarian foreign policy on the eve of World War I, and a two-volume biography of Metternich. His book on the last years of Wallenstein's life was first published in 1920, but a revised edition appeared in 1952. As Srbik himself admits, it was written primarily to refute Pekař.

Wallenstein's significance as a strategist; his far greater standing as the organizer of an army; . . . his creativity in the administration of his lands, in economic policy and public education; his fight for religious toleration in a time of bloody struggles between religious opponents, for the liberation of the German people from foreign saviors who had become oppressors, and for universal respect for the German name—in all these areas the picture is clear, the outline of his personality is sharply and grandly etched. All the same, two of the central problems of this great life will perhaps never be solved definitively—the "guilt question," . . . and the closely related question of what kind of mind the Friedländer had. . . .

One cannot understand Wallenstein's true greatness if, [like Pekař,] one pictures him only as a passionate but irresolute gambler. . . . One cannot throw enough light into the depths of a great and powerful man's nature if one calls him "a weakling crushed by physical afflictions, confused by superstitions, impelled by titanic and megalomanic schemes of revenge, a cowardly traitor, and a foolish intriguer." . . . Is it sufficient to call the organizer, endowed with genius, who created and led an army, a politician "who was not quite normal"? . . .

From Heinrich Ritter von Srbik, *Wallensteins Ende: Ursachen, Verlauf und Folgen der Katastrophe* (Salzburg, 1952), pp. 19–20, 35–36, 41–49, 52, 59–60, 72–73, and 281. Reprinted by permission of Dr. Jur. Hans Heinrich Ritter von Srbik. Editor's translation.

In Wallenstein were embodied the fateful forces of his time. He belonged to the men of the Renaissance and the world of the Baroque, but he also stood above these categories as an exceptional individual. He went beyond Czech or German nationality, beyond Catholic or Protestant denominations. . . . He was a Bohemian and a prince of the German Empire. He concerned himself with the dream of the Bohemian crown far more as an endeavor unconnected with his own person than as a personal ambition, but he was also inspired by a great dream of freedom for the Empire. He was a believer in the starry heavens in an age of religious wars. He stood as an individualistic Machiavellian against absolutism. As Imperial Commander under military oath, he was guilty of attempted treason against the Emperor, but he moved towards complete defection only when he had to fight for his own life. Had his treason succeeded, he might perhaps have been counted among the heroes by a historiography partial to success. Whether one admires or attacks him, one cannot fathom his aims by referring only to ambition and the desire for vengeance. Nor does a struggle for power or the intrigues of a foolish traitor provide a satisfactory analysis of his spirit, if at the same time the shining strength of living faith and living love is completely missed. It is impossible to grasp his nature by using penetrating acuteness or the tools of logic alone. They are insufficient for an understanding of the demon that drove this man, who was a condottiere, but grew to be much more than a condottiere; who was impelled from within and by his contemporaries to inconsistent actions; but who nonetheless followed a fixed and grand design. One can understand Pekař himself admitting that he "cannot find" an answer to the question of Wallenstein's motives in the fall of 1632 and the fall of 1633, that he "cannot rightly understand them." . . . [Wallenstein's personality] was never free of dark areas. He was never one of those great, idealistic figures of history who rise above their own egos; and yet he did rise above mere egoism to the great realization that Germany needed peace, unity, and a just equality for Christian denominations, if the country was not to fall apart as the battleground of Europe in a war on two fronts that nobody could win. However firmly Wallenstein is rooted by Pekař in the tragic history of Bohemia, this Bohemian nobleman belongs just as much to the tragic history of the German people and Empire. . . .

The life of the Bohemian nobleman, Albrecht von Waldstein [Wallenstein], resembles a meteor in its unmatched, glittering rise and its precipitous decline. Posterity has divided his life into two main sections, separated by the first fall of a dimly glowing star at its zenith: the Diet of Regensburg in the year 1630. All the same, the uniformity of an inconsistent yet comprehensive ego, and the identity of a basic political theory, united across the years the victor of the Dessau bridge, the creator of the Peace of Lübeck, the general of the Oceanic and Baltic seas, . . . the loser at Lützen, and the ruined man who fell at the hands of a murderer in Eger on the 26th of February 1634. During both his first and second generalships this man, who was full of emotion and was betrayed by his passions into measureless fury, hatred and sudden impulses, was also a great planner with cool political sense and a suspicious man, a master of "dissimulation" scornful of others. The strength of his resolution did not match the greatness of his political aims, and he had richer abilities as an organizer than as a general. He understood the power of money as did few in his time, and he changed from being one of the most daring speculators during the years of property revolution in his native land to being a genial steward of his creation, the Dukedom of Friedland, and an admirable mercantilistic administrator and developer of his fabulous riches.

He was a magician who created virtually out of nothing a powerful army which saved the House of Austria from disaster and took him to glittering success. He was the terrible master of the principle of forced contributions and the principle that war had to support itself. And he was also the sternest of disciplinarians. Yet he was a prudent, cautious strategist, who never sought a battle, but undertook it only when it was unavoidable, and then turned to iron in the moment of decision. And what about his political goal, which can never be separated from his self-interest, and which rose only late and imperfectly above the particular to the general? During the first generalship this "territoriless" prince, to whom investiture with the Dukedom of Mecklenburg brought weapons, considered the Imperial cause to be much greater than, and opposed to, the liberties of the German princes. An Empire that stretched from the Baltic and the North Sea to the Adriatic should be controlled by a strong Imperial

central government, based on the might of the Hapsburgs' hereditary lands and a powerful army that was raised to provincial status
above the claims of sovereignty of the territorial princes. Such a
government could keep out the influence of foreign powers and with
this unified force it could settle the Byzantine Imperial crown con-
clusively on the head of the Roman-German Emperor. . . . Europe
should overpower Turkey, the eastern Rome, and give a new order to
eastern Europe. . . . This dream of gigantic proportions, born out of
calm reason and the most daring flight of fancy, was a dream of an
Emperor with a national commander and statesman as the real center of gravity. . . .

In his dismissal of Wallenstein, an act of ingratitude and disregard
for political conditions at a time when French, Dutch and above all
Swedish troops stood on German soil, one can see the original cause
of the tragic events of 1634. There now entered into the plans of the
Friedländer, instead of the Imperial cause, more and more the im-
personal—though bound up with personal—cause of the other
branch of that united and contradictory duality, "Emperor and Empire": the Empire.

The Friedländer's pride was deeply hurt and he was filled with an
ardent desire for revenge. Now that the possibility of his leading the
Empire under the seal of the Emperor had disappeared, he considered himself fully a prince of the Empire with the right to control
his own policy and to wage war free from his military oath to Ferdinand. He joined that group of the Bohemian aristocracy which, both
in exile and at home, occupied itself with hopes of restoring the
political, religious and economic conditions that had existed before
the shattering defeat on the White Mountain, before the severe and
dreadful Counter Reformation, before the overthrow of all forms of
property, and before the deportation of the aristocracy. . . . They
wanted to restore the free election of the King of Bohemia, . . . [and]
they counted on help from Gustavus Adolphus, but they needed a
military leader with a far-resounding name, a man of the pride and
confidence who would be capable of ruling the masses. Their hopes
were tied to their compatriot, the Duke of Friedland, . . . who seemed
to be capable and worthy of wearing the crown of the kingdom, if he
were ready to combine his own lofty aspirations with their more

immediate aims. They saw themselves as occupying the middle ground between the foreign powers hostile to the Emperor and the revolution hoped for in Bohemia. . . .

In the summer of 1631 the humiliated and dismissed commander began a double game. . . . He made his first effort to get the Emperor to place him at the head of a Hapsburg army again; but at the same time the vengeance seeker lent his ear to the émigrés and allowed his uncontrollable temper to unleash imprecations and threats which the calmer reflection of other hours denied. . . . The Friedländer played with treason against his previous commander-in-chief and his overlord, but he never went as far as complete treason. . . . How much that is false was asserted about this irresolute man after his horrible end! The Swedish King is supposed to have offered him the crown of Bohemia, and the Friedländer to have demanded the right to issue decrees in all conquered lands! In truth it seems that Gustavus Adolphus at most envisioned a vice-kingship of Bohemia for the Duke. . . . In November 1631 . . . [Wallenstein] had not yet quite given up thoughts of a possible revolution, just as at that time he had also shown no great hurry to reconquer Prague; but now his significant and objective ideal of peace was beginning to take clear shape, though it was still "an ideal plan," whose concrete terms would come only with time. . . . The ideal included the revocation of the Edict of Restitution [and] the reestablishment of the situation in the Empire as it had been in 1618. . . .

It seems to me unacceptable to consider the desire for vengeance and power as the only motive behind Wallenstein's decision [to accept the generalship the second time]. We ought rather to distinguish between a satisfied and a dissatisfied spirit. The hatred of Bavaria undoubtedly remained. . . . Yet even the hostile analysis of a Josef Pekař cannot deny the sincerity and energy of his effort in the early part of 1632 to convert the Elector of Saxony, the Imperial Commander, to peace. To be sure, Pekař also believes that the Duke's plans for peace were no more than plans for revolution against the Emperor. . . . The contention that the reinstated general did not seriously contemplate peace, when he envisioned restoring the Empire "in pristinum statum," lacks convincing proof. . . . Only by distortion can the Duke's words of peace be explained as mere "talk" or "pretext"—as a purely self-seeking fight against the Emperor and his allies; as a plan to destroy the House of Austria with Sweden's help, and to force acceptance of the "Bohemian approach" to peace as opposed to Arnim's "German approach." The real tragedy lies in the fact that it became increasingly clear to Wallenstein after he was once again named Imperial Commander, that he would never be able to achieve his plan for peace with the Emperor's approval, but only by rebellion and treason against his commander-in-chief. With his hesitating, uncertain ways, he was never able to resolve this thorny dilemma, a dilemma which eventually destroyed him. . . .

Soon after the battle of Lützen the dichotomy between Wallenstein's conduct for and against the Emperor reappeared. . . . If he was not to lose Ferdinand's trust, and thus create much too early the greatest obstacles to his plans for peace, then he had to pacify the Emperor and try to win his trust by an act of arms. Only then could he pursue his two-sided policy, which hoped to restore religious peace and the old situation in the Empire, to attract the armies of both Electors [Saxony and Brandenburg], and in an extreme might even lead to an alliance with the Swedes, the French, and the Bohemian conspirators so as to make the head of the Empire and his House accept the peace by force or else to expel them [the Hapsburgs] from the Empire, and then to use the united powers of the Empire to chase the foreigners off its soil. . . .

The great man's own failings and the intrigues of his enemies in Vienna and in the field worked together to bring him to his unfortunate end. . . . The military and political conduct of the Duke, who lacked so much that is necessary for a really great statesman, made it much easier for his political enemies, who were only feebly counter-balanced by his friends, to picture his last projects as very great dangers, both in potential and in fact, to the Hapsburgs and the Catholic Church. The structure was built on sand, and this much-discussed, but irresolute and never fully worked out policy, which convinced nobody and made everyone suspicious, could never have reached its goal. . . .

Since his murder at Eger, the German people have become aware of the inner greatness of the man. They feel that the great idealist became a sacrifice to hostile powers who opposed a rapid peace and who controlled the undecided Emperor. This belief is inseparable from their memory of the great, calamitous war. The people do not consider it a justifiable retribution that disloyalty was defeated by disloyalty, that a traitor should have been killed by treason. For they know instinctively that the dead man's treason was ennobled by a most worthy goal. The majority of the people, tired of religious disputes, of self-flagellation and oppression by foreigners, saw an ideal even higher than the Emperor's—the ideal of peace and fruitful labor that was undermined by the Friedländer's death. And in fact Wallenstein devoted all the power of his mighty spirit, after a life full of stirring deeds, to this ideal, to which he sacrificed his deathly ill body a short time before his natural demise. He died as he was trying with insufficient strength to accelerate that great process of world history in which the Hapsburg-Catholic universalism of the age of the Counter Reformation was replaced by the ideal of equal rights for Christian denominations and the right of states to political self-determination. The German people have understood this instinctively but confusedly, and for this reason the Wallenstein question has never been laid to rest.

Cardinal Richelieu

Cardinal Richelieu
POLITICAL TESTAMENT

Armand Jean du Plessis, Cardinal et Duc de Richelieu (1585–1642) was Louis XIII's chief minister from 1624 until his death. His role in the struggle between France and the encircling Hapsburgs was crucial, because the wars he started (which are traditionally viewed as the "French stage" of the Thirty Years' War) were to end in conspicuous success at the Treaties of Westphalia and the Pyrenees. Nearly all assessors of Richelieu's aims have taken as their starting point the book known as the Testament Politique, *from which the following extracts have been taken. First published in 1688, the authenticity of the* Testament *has been in dispute ever since. The most recent and convincing view holds that, although Richelieu himself did not actually write the* Testament, *it consists of a collection of writings taken from his papers. It thus contains a conglomeration of ideas that Richelieu either expressed or considered, and though not assembled in its present form until after his death, it can with justification be considered a fairly accurate representation of his views. (See Rémy Pithon's article, "A propos du testament politique de Richelieu" in* Revue Suisse d'Histoire, *Vol. 6 (1956), pp. 177–214.) The first extract comes from the review of the reign at the beginning of the* Testament, *and the second is taken from the main part of the* Testament, *where general principles are expounded. (It should be noted that the King, to whom the following is addressed, is sometimes referred to as "you," sometimes as "he" or "him.")*

I

When Your Majesty decided to give me . . . a large part of his confidence in the guidance of his affairs, . . . foreign alliances were badly made, private interests were preferred to public ones, and, in a word, the dignity of the royal majesty was so disgraced and so far from what it should have been, due to the failings of those who principally conducted your affairs at that time, that it was almost im-

From Richelieu's *Testament Politique*. This selection has been taken from Louis André's edition (Paris, 1947), pp. 93–95, 116–119, 134–136, 143–146, 148–149, 347–348, 352, 354–355, 372–373, 375, 379, 381–385, and 388. Editor's translation.

possible to recognize. I could not continue the conduct of those to whom Your Majesty had confided the guidance of his state without losing everything; but, on the other hand, I also could not change direction suddenly "without violating the principles of prudence which do not permit a switch from one extreme to another without passing through middle ground first." . . .

Despite all the difficulties that I laid before Your Majesty, I dared to promise you, without thinking my advice rash, and knowing what Kings could accomplish if they used their power well, that you would find a remedy for the disorders of the state, and that your wisdom, your power, and the blessing of God would in a short space of time give a new appearance to this kingdom. I promised him to use all my industry, and all the authority he would be pleased to give me . . . to reduce all his subjects to their duty and to revive his name among foreign nations to the level at which it deserves to be. . . .

[At the Diet of Ratisbon] the discontent felt toward the Emperor and the Spaniards by the Duke of Bavaria, who until then had been inseparably attached to the House of Austria, and the fear felt by all the Electors, both Catholic and Protestant, that they would be deprived of their estates, as many other princes had already been by the Emperor's [Edict of Restitution], made them secretly seek your support. You negotiated with them so adroitly and with so much success that they prevented, in the presence of the Emperor himself, the election of the King of the Romans, even though the Diet of Ratisbon had been convoked for this sole reason.

Then, to please Bavaria, to satisfy the Electors and various other princes, and to fortify all of them in their resolution to make the Catholic League independent, not of the Emperor, but of Spain, which was usurping its leadership, your ambassadors . . . helped these princes to depose Wallenstein from the command of the armies of the Empire (which helped not a little to slow down the affairs of his master). . . .

A little later the King of Sweden embarked on his enterprise to prevent the oppression of the princes of the Empire in Germany, and this plan was no sooner known to you than Your Majesty, to prevent any prejudice to the Catholic religion, concluded a treaty with him which obliged him not to disturb its exercise in any of the areas of his conquests.

I know well that your enemies, who hope to justify their actions by criticizing yours, have overlooked nothing in their effort to make this agreement seem odious. But their plan has had no effect other than to reveal their malice. The innocence of Your Majesty is absolutely clear, because his ambassador did not enter into any treaty with this conqueror until he had been in Germany for six months. This easily proves that the treaties made with this prince were the remedy for the wrong and not its cause.

The treaties concluded not only with this great King, but also with many other princes of Germany, were justified anyway because they were absolutely necessary for the safety of the Duke of Mantua, who had been unjustly attacked, and for the security of all Italy, over which the Spaniards had no less right than they did over the lands of this poor prince, since they considered their convenience sufficient legitimacy. . . .

If it is an action of singular wisdom to have kept all the forces of the enemies of your state occupied for ten years by the armies of your allies, using your treasury and not your weapons, then, when your allies could no longer survive on their own, it was an act of both courage and wisdom to enter into open war. This shows that, in managing the security of the kingdom, you have acted like those stewards who, having been careful to save money, know when to spend it to prevent a greater loss. . . .

You attacked in various places at the same time . . . in order to keep your enemies occupied on all sides so that they could be invincible in none.

The war in Germany was virtually unavoidable, since this part of Europe had been the theater where it had opened long before.

Although the war in Flanders did not achieve the success one might have expected, it was impossible not to regard it as advantageous in its aims.

The war in the Grisons was necessary so as to encourage the Italian princes to take up arms by removing their fear of the Germans. . . .

The war in Italy was no less important, as much because this was the best way to get the Duke of Savoy on our side, as because the Milanese, the heart of the states possessed by Spain, was the territory he had to attack.

As for the rest, if one considers that Your Majesty had allies on all sides who had to join forces with you, it is common sense that the Spaniards, attacked in various places by .such a union, would succumb under the force of your power. . . .

During the course of this war . . . nothing went wrong for you without seeming to have happened only for your glory. . . .

Various things are worthy of note about this war.

The first is that Your Majesty did not enter the war until it was unavoidable, and did not leave it until he had to. This observation sheds great glory on Your Majesty, because when at peace France was often urged by its allies to take up arms, though reluctant to do so. And during the war his enemies often proposed a separate peace, but he would never consider it because France could not be separated from the interests of its allies.

Those who know that Your Majesty was abandoned by several princes allied to France, and that nonetheless he did not wish to abandon anyone; that moreover some of those who remained loyal let him down in several important matters, yet still received from Your Majesty the treatment they were promised; those people, I say, understand that if the good fortune of Your Majesty is apparent in the success of his endeavors, his virtue is no less great than his good fortune. I know well that if France had broken its word, its reputation would have suffered badly, and the least loss of this kind means that a great prince has nothing further to lose. But it was no small matter to have lived up to one's obligations on various occasions when the natural desire for vengeance and peace after a war gave way to an opposite course of action.

You needed wisdom no less than force, an effort of will no less than one of arms, to persevere almost alone in those very designs which you had hoped would succeed by the union of many. . . .

The second observation on this subject worthy of great note is that Your Majesty did not, so as to protect himself from the peril of war, expose Christianity to Ottoman arms, which were often offered to us.

He was not unaware that he could have accepted such assistance with justification. Yet this knowledge was not strong enough to make him take a step which endangered religion, however advantageous it might have been for securing peace.

The example of some of his predecessors, and various princes of the House of Austria, who especially try to appear as religious before God as he is in fact in his private beliefs, was too weak to carry him into what history teaches us has been practiced by others a number of times. . . .

If I add that his many preoccupations did not prevent him from properly fortifying, at the same time, all his frontiers, which previously had been open on all sides to his enemies, then their present state can only be cause for astonishment. It will be an innovation no less important to posterity that, having gained security forever, this kingdom will in the future gather as many of the fruits of Your Majesty's labors and efforts as he has received in the past.

Those to whom history will reveal the crosses Your Majesty encountered in all his great designs: through the envy his successes, and the fear his power, aroused among various princes, including occasionally some of his allies; through the disloyalty of his evil subjects; through a brother badly advised; through a mother always possessed of evil intentions; . . . they will realize that such obstacles have in no small way increased your glory, and they will realize also that great courage cannot be diverted by the difficulties it encounters.

If they consider further the natural frivolity of this nation, the impatience of its soldiers who are little accustomed to hard work, and finally the weakness of the instruments which by necessity you had to use on these occasions—among which I hold the first place —they will have to admit that nothing made up for the failings of your implements except the excellence of Your Majesty, who was the artisan.

Finally, if they realize that after overcoming all these obstacles you succeeded in concluding a peace, in which . . . you returned territory that you yourself had conquered, they cannot fail to realize that your generosity equals your power, and in your conduct wisdom and the blessing of God march side by side. . . .

II

One cannot imagine how many advantages states gain from continued negotiations, if conducted wisely, unless one has experienced it oneself. I admit I did not realize this truth for five or six years after being employed in the management of policy. But I am now so sure of it that I dare to say boldly that to negotiate everywhere without cease, openly and secretly, even though one makes no immediate gains, and future gains seem unlikely, is absolutely necessary for the good of the state. . . .

He who negotiates all the time will find at last the right moment to achieve his aims, and even if he does not find it, at least it is true that he can lose nothing, and that through his negotiations he knows what is happening in the world, which is of no small consequence for the good of the state. . . .

Important negotiations must not be interrupted for a moment. One must pursue one's aims with unfailing intensity. . . . One must not be disheartened by an unfortunate turn of events, because sometimes it happens that what is undertaken with good reason is achieved with little good fortune.

It is difficult to fight often and always win. . . . It is often because negotiations are so innocent that one can gain great advantages from them without ever faring badly. . . .

In matters of state one must find an advantage in everything; that which can be useful must never be neglected.

Leagues are of this nature. The profit is often uncertain, but all the same one must not belittle them. Yet I would never advise a great prince to embark voluntarily on the foundation of a league for a purpose whose execution is difficult, unless he considers himself strong enough to succeed even if his colleagues desert him. . . .

Kings have to take good care before making treaties, but once made they have to observe them religiously.

I know that much of politics teaches the contrary. But . . . I maintain that, since the loss of one's honor is worse than the loss of one's life, a great prince must sooner risk his own person and the interests of his state than break his word, which cannot be violated without the loss of his reputation, which is the greatest force a sovereign has. . . .

Power is one of the most necessary ingredients of the greatness of kings and the happiness of their rule. . . . The foundation of their power must be esteem and respect. . . . This is so necessary that if their power is based on some other principle, it becomes very dangerous, because instead of causing a reasonable fear, this power creates hatred toward princes, who are never in a worse situation than when they fall into public disfavor. . . .

It is against common sense not to realize how important it is to great states to have their frontiers well equipped and fortified.

This is much more necessary in this kingdom where, although the frivolity of our nation renders us incapable of great conquests, its courage makes it invincible in defense if it has places so well fortified and armed that it can make its valor felt. . . . The most powerful state in the world cannot boast of enjoying guaranteed peace unless it is capable of protecting itself at all times from an unexpected invasion or surprise attack. . . .

One must be capable of waging a long war, should the good of the state require it. In the judgement of men of the highest repute, war is sometimes an unavoidable evil and, in some circumstances, it is absolutely necessary and may even achieve some good.

States need war at certain times to purge themselves of their evil humors, to recover what belongs to them, to avenge an injury which, if unpunished, would invite a second, to protect their allies from oppression, to halt the advance and pride of a conqueror, to forestall evils which apparently threaten and which one does not know how to evade any other way, or finally for various other reasons. . . .

There is no nation in the world less inclined to war than our own. The frivolity and impatience evident in our least efforts are two characteristics which overwhelmingly confirm, to my great regret, this observation. . . .

If [the French had the military skill] to accompany their valor, the universe would not be big enough to accommodate all their conquests. But although the great courage God gave them makes them capable of defeating anyone who opposes them by force, their frivolity and feebleness when faced by hard work makes them incapable of overcoming the least of the delays that a cunning enemy would use to fight their ardor.

It follows that they are not suitable for conquests that need time, nor for the preservation of what they conquer in an instant. . . . They have been accused of never being satisfied and of being too little attached to their country. This accusation has so much foundation that one cannot deny that there are more people in France who neglect the obligations they have to the place of their birth than there are in all the nations of the world. . . .

More than anyone else, they are blinded by their own successes and lose heart and judgement in adversity and difficulties. . . .

[Yet] the French are capable of anything, provided their commanders are capable of teaching them well what they have to do.

Aldous Huxley

THE LUST FOR POWER AND MONEY

Aldous Huxley (1894–1963) was a member of a distinguished English family— his grandfather was the famous biologist who defended Darwin's theories. Educated at Eton and Balliol College, Oxford, he began his career by working on magazines, writing poetry and drama criticism. A brilliant satirist, he made a great success with his novel Antic Hay, *published in 1923. Many other novels and essays followed, perhaps the most famous being the scathing satire of a scientific Utopia,* Brave New World *(1932). His one major venture into history was a highly readable and emotional biography of Richelieu's close associate, the Capuchin Father Joseph, which appeared in 1941 under the title* Grey Eminence. *The selection that follows gives a good idea of the approach typically taken by those hostile to Richelieu, and it provides a revealing contrast to the largely favorable view held by most historians and typified, below, by Batiffol and Tapié. It is interesting that some of the most pronounced attacks have come, not from historians, but from literary men like Huxley—others in this company include Victor Hugo, Hilaire Belloc, and of course Alexandre Dumas. Perhaps it is easier to see Richelieu as a symbol of evil than to discover his evil on closer examination.*

Richelieu . . . was . . . a [good] Frenchman, . . . but in that age many good Frenchmen did not scruple to accept substantial gifts and pensions from foreign governments. The current conventions of honor and morality did not unequivocally condemn such practices, which were common among the aristocracies of every country

From pp. 164–166 and 172–177 of *Grey Eminence* by Aldous Huxley. Copyright 1941 by Aldous Leonard Huxley. Reprinted by permission of Harper and Row, Publishers, Incorporated, and Chatto and Windus Ltd.

in Europe. This being so, Richelieu would quite probably have seen no reason for refusing such a gift, all the more so as he would not have felt bound by it to keep his side of the bargain. He could have taken the bribe with a good social and political conscience. As for his personal conscience, that would not have been troubled even for a moment. He felt no scruples about money and could indulge his covetousness without a qualm. Such scruples as he had were mainly sexual. He had a high opinion of continence—no doubt because he had a low opinion of women. "These animals," he said of them, "are very strange. One sometimes thinks they must be incapable of doing much harm, because they are incapable of doing any good; but I protest on my conscience that there is nothing so well able to ruin a state as they are." Belial, it is evident, was no more dangerous to the Cardinal than to the friar [Father Joseph]. But when it came to Mammon, the demon of wealth, and Lucifer, the arch-fiend of pride and power, the case was very different. Richelieu was eaten up by a consuming lust for power. Nor was the reality of power enough; he also desired the appearance of it. There is a story that his uncle, La Porte, was present at a meeting between Richelieu and the Duke of Savoy, when the former took precedence over the latter and, as they walked along, passed first through every doorway. "To think," exclaimed the old gentleman in a kind of rapturous *Nunc Dimittis,* "to think that I should have seen the grandson of lawyer La Porte walking in front of the grandson of [the Emperor] Charles V!" Behind that cold, impassive mask of his, the Cardinal rejoiced as whole-heartedly as his bourgeois uncle. These triumphs were profoundly important to him.

No less important were the triumphs he could buy with money —the palaces, the attendants, the plate, the libraries, the great banquets, the gorgeous masques for which bishops acted as choreographers, and the audience consisted of queens and princes, great nobles and ambassadors. The passion for wealth was born and bred in him, and grew with every satisfaction it received. His speech before the States General in 1614 contains a passage which his subsequent behavior was to render exquisitely comic. Expatiating on the desirability of employing priests in the affairs of state, he declared that the clergy "are freer than other men from the private interests which so often harm the public. Observing celibacy, they

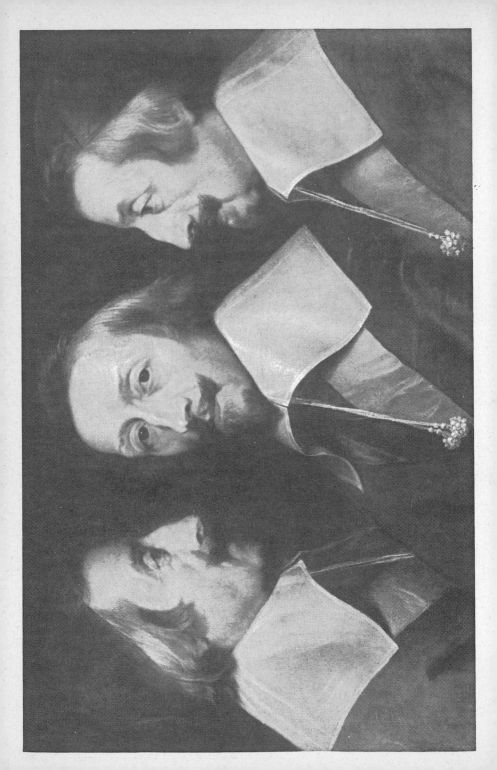

have nothing to survive them but their souls, and these do not accumulate earthly treasures." By 1630, the speaker was in receipt of an income of fifteen hundred thousand livres from the accumulation of ecclesiastical benefices alone. His salaries, perquisites and miscellaneous pickings amounted to four or five millions more. Of the grand total, he spent upon himself four million livres (the annual subsidy given by France to her Swedish allies was less than a million), and he put aside at the end of each year enough to make it possible for him to leave to his nephews and nieces an estate valued in the scores of millions. When one considers that the purchasing power of a livre in the early seventeenth century amounted to seven or eight gold francs, one is forced to admit that, for a man whose profession discouraged him from "accumulating earthly treasures," the Cardinal did not do too badly.

Money and power were not the only "manlier objects" for which Richelieu yearned. He also had an itch for literary fame. He employed a committee of five poets to work up his ideas into dramatic form, and when one of them, Corneille, wrote *Le Cid,* the Cardinal was consumed by envy and, through paid critics, tried to prove that the tragedy was entirely undeserving of the praise it had received.

Richelieu's, it is evident from his biography, was a case which can have presented no difficulties to the Tempter. The Satan of *Paradise Regained* is only a shade more intelligent than poor Belial; but to land a pike so frantically greedy as was the Cardinal requires little more than the bare minimum of cunning. Any old "manlier object" was bait enough for Richelieu. . . .

Richelieu shared [Father Joseph's] convictions in regard to France, the monarchy, and the disagreeableness of political labor and the obligations which that very disagreeableness imposed. But whereas these convictions were of prime importance to Father Joseph, to Richelieu they were only a secondary consideration.

FIGURE 5. *Cardinal Richelieu.* This triple portrait by the French painter Phillippe de Champaigne conveys a sense of its subject by allowing one to see both profiles together with the full face. Richelieu is wearing his cardinal's robes, but Champaigne seems to be stressing the character rather than the formality of the man. (*Reproduced by courtesy of the Trustees, The National Gallery, London.*)

Even if France and the monarchy had meant nothing to him, he would still have found, in his native genius, his inordinate lust for power, his passion for money, amply sufficient reasons for going into politics.

Certain passages in the Cardinal's letters and memoirs throw a very interesting light on the matters we have been discussing; for they reveal to us what Richelieu thought about his political activities, in their relation to God, his fellow men and his own salvation. The Cardinal begins by making a sharp distinction between personal and public morality—between what Niebuhr would call "moral men and immoral society." *"Autre chose est être homme de bien selon Dieu et autre chose être tel selon les hommes."*[1] To take a specific example of this difference, the good man according to God must forgive offenses against himself as soon as they are committed; but where offenses have been committed against society, the good man according to men must do everything in his power to take vengeance.

> *The reason for this difference springs from the same principle as applied to two different kinds of obligation. The first and greatest obligation of a man is the salvation of his soul, which demands that vengeance should be left to God and not taken by the person offended. The greatest obligation of kings is the repose of their subjects, the preservation in its entirety of their state, and of the reputation of their government; to which end it is necessary to punish all offenses against the state so effectively that the severity of the vengeance may remove the very thought of renewing the injury.*

Richelieu himself was a representative of the King and an *homme de bien selon les hommes.* This being so, it was not legitimate for him to behave as an *homme de bien selon Dieu,* even though failure so to behave might imperil his chances of eternal bliss. His view of himself was at bottom very similar to that which the more tender-minded of communist sympathizers often take of Lenin—that of a kind of secular savior, taking upon himself the responsibility for intrinsically evil acts, which he performs, with full knowledge of their consequences for himself, in order to ensure the future happiness of mankind. "Many men," wrote the Cardinal, "would save

---

[1] "To be a good man according to God is one thing; to be a good man according to men is quite another."—Ed.

their souls as private persons who damn themselves as public persons." To benefit the French people (if not at the moment, at any rate at some future time), to increase the power and glory of France, as personified in her kings, he was prepared to run the appalling risk of going to hell. And his punishment was not reserved exclusively for the next world; like all statesmen, he was called upon, here and now, to accept a frightful burden of fatigues and scruples and anxieties. He was one who, in his own memorable phrase, "lies awake at night that others may sleep fearlessly in the shadow of his watchings"—"à l'ombre de ses veilles." In this heroic self-portrait there is, of course, an element of truth; but it is very far from being the whole truth. In describing himself as a Promethean savior, a voluntary scapegoat suffering for the sake of the people, Richelieu omitted to mention those little items of the five-million-a-year income, the dukedom, the absolute power, the precedence over princes of the blood, the fawnings and flatteries of all who approached him. "Verily, they have their reward." . . .

So much for motives and their rationalizations. In temperament . . . Richelieu . . . had no enthusiasm, only a fixed intensity of purpose. Inspirations and happy intuitions played little or no part in his life; everything he did was planned and calculated for the sole purpose of bringing, not indeed the greatest happiness to the greatest number, but the greatest advantage to Armand Du Plessis de Richelieu and the greatest glory to France. . . . There was madness in the family. Richelieu's elder brother—the Carthusian monk, whom he dragged out of his monastery and made the Cardinal-Archbishop of Lyon—was not merely feeble-minded; he also suffered every now and then from delusions of grandeur, believing himself to be the First Person of the Trinity. Richelieu himself is known to have been a victim to fits of morbid depression and occasional explosions of rage, almost epileptic in their violence. Furthermore, a tradition was preserved in the royal family that, like his brother, he was sometimes subject to delusions. But whereas the poor half-wit thought of himself as God, the arrogant, self-deified genius was doomed, by a stroke of beautifully poetic justice, to be convinced that he was less than human. In his spells of mental aberration, the Cardinal imagined himself to be a horse.

These psychological lesions were not, however, so serious that they prevented Richelieu from doing his work. He did it with the efficiency, which is possible only to those who possess, as well as the highest intellectual abilities, an extraordinary strength and fixity of resolution.

Few men will anything very strongly, and out of these few, only a tiny minority are capable of combining strength of will with unwavering continuity. Most human beings are spasmodic and intermittent creatures, who like above everything the pleasures of mental indolence. "It is for this reason," says Bryce, "that a strenuous and unwearying will sometimes becomes so tremendous a power, almost a hypnotic force." Lucifer is the highest mythological incarnation of this intense personal will, and the great men who have embodied it upon the stage of history participate, to some extent, in his satanic strength and magnificence. It is because of this strength and magnificence, so very different from our own weakness and mental squalor, that we continue to hark back nostalgically to the biographies of such men as Alexander, Caesar, Napoleon, and that, as each new imitator of Lucifer arises, we prostrate ourselves before him, begging him to save us. And, of course, many of these Great Men would genuinely like to save their fellows. But since they are what they are, not saints, but petty Lucifers, their well-meant efforts can lead only to the perpetuation, in some temporarily less or more unpleasant form, of those conditions from which humanity is perpetually praying to be saved. Great Men have invariably failed to "deliver the goods"; but because we admire their qualities and envy their success, we continue to believe in them and to submit to their power. At the same time, we know quite well, with a part of our being, that Lucifers cannot possibly do us any good; so we turn for a moment from such incarnations of the personal will to those very different human beings, who incarnate the will of God. The Saints are even more willing to help than the Great Men; but the advice they give is apt to seem depressing to men and women who want to enjoy the pleasures of indolence. "God," says the Saints, "helps those who help themselves"; and they go on to prescribe the methods by which it is possible to help oneself. But we don't want to have to help ourselves; we want to be helped, to have somebody who will do the work on our behalf. So we turn back again to the incarnations of the personal will. These Great Men have not the smallest doubt of their ability to give us exactly what we want —a political system that will make everybody happy and good, a state religion that guarantees God's favors here on earth and a blissful eternity in paradise. We accept their offer; and immediately the other part of our being reverts to the Saints, from whom once again we turn to our disastrous Great Men. And so it goes on, century after century. The pathetic shilly-shallying has left its accumulated traces in our libraries, where the records of Great Men and their activities in history fill about as much shelf-room as the records of the Saints and their dealings with God.

Richelieu was one of the great incarnations of the personal will. It was to his never relaxed inflexibility of purpose that he owed his extraordinary career, and by means of which he was able to stamp his impress so profoundly upon the history of Europe. . . .

Louis Batiffol

A POLICY OF JUSTICE, NECESSITY, AND TRADITION

Louis Batiffol (1865–1946) was born in Toulouse. After receiving his doctorate he worked in the Bibliothèque Nationale de France from 1890 to 1924. He never held an academic post, but during his years in the library he devoted himself to research in the history of France in the early seventeenth century. His knowledge of the period was unmatched, and at the library he was able to explore a tremendous literature of little-known tracts and pamphlets. The books he wrote helped reshape the history of Louis XIII's reign. They ranged from studies of the Louvre and of Paris to works on Louis XIII, Marie de Medici, Richelieu and Cardinal de Retz. The extracts that follow come from his book on Richelieu and King Louis XIII *published in 1934.*

On every side one seems convinced that as a minister Richelieu worked only for France and the King, and nothing else. The Queen Mother could exult at the success of her protégé. But if she imagined, wrote the Italian resident Pesaro, that she was going to command power at her whim, she was badly mistaken! The Cardinal

From Louis Batiffol, *Richelieu et le roi Louis XIII* (Paris, 1934), pp. 21, 61–62 and 66–70. Reprinted by permission of Madame Louis Batiffol. Editor's translation.

would serve only the King and the public interest. He probably would even be, the Italian envoy added, more a statesman than a churchman. The author of a tract, *The Voice of the Public to the King,* wrote that henceforth Richelieu would seek no other support but "the legitimate authority of the King" and would not propose any goal but "the good conduct of public affairs." Wise and able, he would be "a good Frenchman." And the Cardinal himself confirmed these prophecies in a note that we have where he says that he intends to apply himself "only to the service of the King and the good of the State, wishing to work for it to the last drop of his blood and wanting to die rather than think of some matter which would not be advantageous to the kingdom"! Certainly he "would never betray the Queen Mother," but he would also "do nothing against the service of the King"!

And it was a new Richelieu who appeared, different from the man whom the King and many others had seen, or thought they had seen, up to that time! . . .

He wanted to undertake only those enterprises which would be neither futile nor chimerical, but immediately necessary, pressing and, moreover, attainable. In practice he professed that he had to attend to everything and "benefit from everything," because "in politics," he added, "one is guided more by necessities than by predetermined wishes." This answers the contention . . . that he "intended everything that he did." He had a practical nature, and he acted accordingly. Let us look briefly at the grand projects that have been attributed to him.

The idea of the attainment of France's "natural frontiers" has been attributed to him. I have shown . . . with regard to Alsace that his fundamental thinking, like that of all the jurists of the time, was that the King could hope to acquire only those territories to which he had some rights, established by undoubted titles, privileges of sovereignty (as in Lorraine), inheritance, grant, purchase or treaty. These jurists . . . had drawn up solid dissertations for him, which we possess, where the regions France was legitimately entitled to claim through various titles are enumerated: Lorraine, the Franche-Comté, Artois, Flanders, and even stranger territories such as the Milanese, Naples and Sicily. The Rhine area and Alsace never figured in these lists. The jurists did not talk of natural frontiers.

They did not think of invoking this title and Richelieu did not speak of it at all. . . . Without a doubt he knew the right of conquest, the right of war, but he thought . . . that this right "is neither established nor plausible," and that in any case it was not worthy of the Most Christian King, surnamed "the Just," to invoke such a right, and he would not stoop to it. In fact in his papers we see that he fixed as "war aims" the breaking of all juridical ties between the German Empire and Lorraine and the three bishoprics of Metz, Toul and Verdun, so as to incorporate them into France. At the Treaty of Westphalia Mazarin was to obtain the three bishoprics, but substituted Alsace for Lorraine. . . .

In foreign affairs Richelieu wanted the governments of Europe to have toward France "the consideration they ought to have to so great a State." On the other side the King would act justly toward them, and practice "strict justice." And "strict justice," said the Cardinal, consisted of "never attacking but always defending oneself against the enterprises of one's enemies, because, in following this path, God is with us!"

What has been called the Cardinal's "grand policy" toward the House of Austria was not invented by him. This policy had been a necessity for a century for all the governments that had succeeded one another in France since the day Charles V, King of Spain, became the Emperor of the German Holy Roman Empire and thus encircled the King with his possessions and threatened to stifle him. Our kings of the sixteenth century saw clearly that they had an obligation to free themselves of this grip, even after the separation of Spain from the Empire after the abdication of Charles V (the two branches of the House of Austria remained united in policy). . . . In 1603 Henri IV had explained that the House of Austria, by its position in Europe, threatened the whole world with "universal domination"; that France and England had to stay united to resist this domination; that one had to support the Netherlands, who had revolted in hopes of independence from Spain to whom they belonged; and that he had good cause to help and ally with the Protestant princes in Germany who opposed the Catholic Emperor, from whom they had everything to fear. This was exactly Richelieu's policy, formulated word for word before his time. Events controlled him. . . . The enterprises of the Catholic Emperor Ferdinand II against the Protestant princes in Germany, which attempted to deprive them of their states, expel them, and unite Germany, were going to provide Richelieu with the opportunity for action. He did not let it escape.

At the start of 1629 he established the uniquely defensive character of his action in accordance with his principles: "to halt the advance of the House of Austria." For this—and here are the precise details of the plan of execution he set up—"France," he said, "had to think first of fortifying itself at home." Then they had to be ready to go to the help of their allies. For this purpose it was most necessary to occupy a few entries into the lands of the enemy, through which one could easily invade the adversary if the circumstances required: Strassburg, for example, which offered access into Germany, . . . Versoix on the Swiss side, Saluces on the Italian side, etc.

The essential principle of maintaining allies everywhere haunted Richelieu constantly. . . . France, he said, was the object of universal jealousy. It could count on nobody. It was perpetually betrayed. But the small states needed and turned to France. This clientele was a power, and one had to attach oneself to it. This would give France a glorious role and was in accord with the positive interests of the kingdom, because it was preferable to support the enemies of one's adversary than to take the sword in hand alone. The pamphleteers accused Richelieu, a Cardinal of the holy Church, of having protected heretics against the Catholic Emperor. But he always replied that he did not act "to help the German Protestants in their pernicious designs against religion," but only "to maintain German liberties" so as to guarantee the security of France. . . .

At the same time as in Germany, Richelieu acted similarly in Italy, where the House of Austria, which possessed the Milanese, threatened to dominate all the states of the peninsula. He declared that a free and independent Italy should belong to the Italians, who had to expel the Germans. "The real secret of Italian affairs," he wrote. . . , "is to deprive the House of Austria of what it holds there, and return the lands to Italian princes and potentates." Then the Italians, so as to protect themselves, would unite and form a league that France would support. . . .

There was nothing in this practical policy, determined as it was solely by the necessities for which one had to prepare for the security of France, that revealed the slightest thought, secret or not, of extending the frontiers of the kingdom to the limits they had reached in Roman times. The Cardinal wrote . . . "I have more desire for a good peace in Christendom than all those who tell you they have such a great longing for it. I serve a master who has no wish whatsoever to increase his territories by despoiling his neighbors. He has never let foreign countries see his arms except in the defense of princes and States who have been unjustly attacked." He repeated that France sought nothing but "the reduction of the House of Austria," this reduction being "the only share," he added, "that France wanted from the entire conquest." These are the general conditions for peace that he wanted to obtain, for what he called "an honorable and certain, a just peace," to be negotiated "in good faith." There was no other. Let us remember that he wrote: "My maxim is to tell frankly what I want and to want only what is reasonable."

Thus the role France played in support and protection of the small states so as to assure both their security and its own, without any idea of an unjustified acquisition of territory that would have been unattainable for numerous juridical, political and other reasons, this was Richelieu's clear, firm and entire purpose.

And it was in the continuous pursuit of this wise, moderate and realistic policy that his incomparable mastery gave to those who saw him close at hand, and to those of his contemporaries who felt its effects, the impression that this was a superior statesman, extraordinary in every way.

V. L. Tapié
THE OVERBURDENED STATESMAN DRIVEN BY EVENTS

Victor L. Tapié, born at Nantes in 1900, studied in Paris and Prague, and after teaching at various French schools, was professor of history at the Univer-

From V. L. Tapié, *La France de Louis XIII et de Richelieu* (Paris, 1952), pp. 379–380, 390–391, 395–396, 398–401, 403–404 and 407–409. Reprinted by permission of Librairie Ernest Flammarion. Editor's translation.

sities of Lille and then Rio de Janeiro. Since 1949 he has been professor of history at the University of Paris. He has travelled frequently to Czechoslovakia, Hungary, Austria, and Russia, and is rare among Western students of the seventeenth century in his knowledge of central and eastern Europe. His earliest work, published in 1934, was a pioneer study of French foreign policy during the early part of the Thirty Years' War. Based on his doctoral thesis, it provided much new material on Bohemia. After a book on nineteenth century Latin America, he returned to French history and the reign of Louis XIII, publishing in 1952 the work from which the following selection is taken. In recent years he has produced two books on Baroque art.

With the death of Gustavus Adolphus everything could have changed in Europe. Would the coalition animated by the King of Sweden now dissolve, though unconquered by Wallenstein? Would not then the reestablishment of peace in the Empire set Spain free to attack France at leisure? Richelieu saw the danger. He knew he had to guard the kingdom against any threat of invasion from the Netherlands or the east. . . .

Wallenstein, too, foundered in turn like Gustavus Adolphus. . . . France and the Hapsburgs stood face to face in Europe, the only protagonists capable of pursuing a policy. It became more and more difficult for Richelieu to postpone France's entry into the conflict if he was not to hasten the collapse of the Protestant party and the victory of the imperialists. . . . Peace negotiations had resumed in Germany . . . [and] Richelieu knew that everything would definitely be lost unless, instead of supporting foreign generals with money, France itself entered the struggle as a combatant. But he was not yet ready. . . .

Richelieu worked to prevent the disorganization of the Protestant leagues in the Empire, but he did not want to enter the war there. To have reinforced the Protestant party in Germany would have prejudiced his general policy, alienated him from German Catholics, bolstered indirectly the prestige of the Emperor, and attracted hostility in France. And if the armies of the King were to penetrate too deeply into a foreign country, they risked being taken for conquerors. . . .

Frederick Henry, Prince of Orange, proposed a combined operation in the Spanish Netherlands and a partition of the conquered territories. Richelieu considered this enterprise dangerous also. He feared future difficulties, should France and the United Provinces become neighboring powers. He preferred a "barrier" between them, established by means of an independent state. He thus already foresaw the solution of a buffer state, a free Belgium. In these difficult times Richelieu's best support came from his remarkable sense of balance. His ambition and daring did not degenerate into megalomania. The weakness of his resources did not discourage him or deter him from action, but he took it into consideration. He avoided the foolhardiness which could have undermined the prestige that France's successes had attained, and he himself was never dazzled by these successes.

There is greater grandeur in these careful preparations—a care that on close examination one is almost tempted to call timidity—than in the brilliant deeds which others in his place would have rushed to perform. His conduct gains a quality of force and humanity that satisfies one's spirit like a classical work of art. . . .

Incessant negotiations occupied the autumn of 1634 and spring of 1635: difficult, laborious, they achieved nothing but compromises. But the essential point was assured: the King of France remained the force behind a coalition still active against the Emperor and Spain, despite the reestablishment of peace in Germany. . . .

France was soon going to enter into open war. In March 1635 Spanish troops took prisoner in Trier the archbishop-elector, Philip of Sötern, even though this prince had placed himself and his city under the protection of Louis XIII. . . . [Yet] Richelieu continued to feel very uneasy about the conditions under which he was entering the conflict. He undoubtedly would have wished to wait even longer, but, because of the insistence of Holland and Sweden, this was no longer possible. . . .

In accepting the pretext that had been offered [the imprisonment of Philip of Sötern], Richelieu was certainly not outmaneuvering his adversaries [who wanted to force him to declare war], but he definitely could use it to pose as the defender of a German prince, and thus as a protector of German liberties, to counter the danger that an offensive in Germany . . . might appear to be an act of provocation. Nor was this the only advantage. He could also attract the Italians to come under French protection, just like the Rhine princes, . . . [and] this policy led to the July 1635 Treaty of Rivoli between France and the Dukes of Savoy and Parma. . . .

Thus the decision to open hostilities . . . was imposed by events, and was not the result of a completely free choice by Richelieu, but it deserves to be called "advantageous in its aims," and "an act of both courage and wisdom." These are the very words Richelieu used to justify it. . . . The war was solemnly declared [by a herald], in the chivalric manner of the Middle Ages, and in the forms of a ceremony that was observed for the last time. . . .

[Thus there began] a twenty-five year war (1635–1659) between France and Spain. It was undoubtedly a fratricidal conflict between two Christian and Catholic nations, . . . but it was also an inevitable duel, given the current ideas and situation in Europe, between two powers, one of whom was inclined toward hegemony, while the other, under the alternately inexorable and cautious leadership of the Cardinal, was going to defend the integrity of its territories, and despite many contradictions in its conduct, was also going to defend the right of the countries of Europe to have no rulers but their natural princes, which was the liberty of the time. . . .

Richelieu declared war a few weeks after the King of France and the Emperor had given their consent to the opening of negotiations for the reestablishment of a general peace, and he did not at all repudiate these negotiations. This does not mean in any way that he did not intend to pursue the war seriously. Quite the contrary. For he could have no better argument in diplomatic negotiations than a recent victory, which could prove the military might of one power and give the other cause to fear further developments. . . .

One can say that the declaration of war opens a new phase in the history of the reign and the ministry. Neither his *Mémoirs,* nor his *Testament,* nor his correspondence reveals all of Richelieu's thoughts. . . .

One often finds oneself led to the conclusion that the course of events had more of an effect on his policy than not. Besides, it is not to belittle his merits (quite the contrary, perhaps) to recognize, at the distance of centuries, that he by no means completed his program. He would have had to resign himself to perpetual compromises. The wrong that he suppressed at one point would reappear at another. This magnificent constructor of French unity and royal absolutism was far from accomplishing all that he wanted. He often did what he never expected to do, so as to leave behind a life's work which, though of undoubted grandeur, was on many sides incomplete and fragile. One can admit that he always believed he would have to come to open war with Spain at some time or another. But he very probably would have wished to choose his own moment, and not engage in battle without a proven army and a disciplined and approving country. . . .

Indeed, ever since 1630 . . . he had realized that he would have to sacrifice his plans for internal reform to foreign policy. . . . From then on he had devoted all his care to preventing the war in Germany from extending to the frontiers and territory of France. He also accomplished the occupation of Lorraine, which possibly remains, if not his greatest achievement, at least the achievement where his aims were most fully realized. Leaving to Father Joseph and his cohorts the details of negotiations in the complicated affairs of the Empire, . . . he nonetheless followed events in Germany closely, determined not to allow a peace dictated by the Emperor to be reached, and ready to support the adversaries of the House of Austria. Although Richelieu never turned away from Italian affairs, working to encircle the Milanese and to keep Italy outside the Spanish empire, one can see that from about 1632 Germany, the Netherlands and Lorraine occupied a larger and larger place in his concerns.

The health of the Cardinal, mediocre always, injured further by the quacks of the time, was a perpetual obstacle in his work. . . . Under these conditions, what could be more absurd than to imagine that he could be everywhere at the same time, and concern himself with every detail? His role as a minister was one of perpetual negotiation. . . . In order to conduct a general policy, the Cardinal gave combined directives to all those needed for its execution, and then always arbitrated the conflicts. But he had to abandon to his trusted associates what we today would call large sectors. This was particularly so from 1635 on.

Finally, once hostilities commenced, he had neither the time nor the means to think of anything else. . . . Henceforth he was bound to foreign policy, and therefore to the war and diplomacy. . . . He had to get what he could out of men, institutions and practices as he found them, nothing more.

Suggestions for Additional Reading

It would be pointless to attempt to provide, in this limited space, anything like a full bibliography for a subject that comes to include the political, social and economic history of almost all Europe in the first half of the seventeenth century. What follows is a list of a few useful bibliographical guides and some of the more important works on countries, subjects and people closely connected with the problems raised in this book. The emphasis is on the broad, general works and the significant recent monographs which would be the natural starting-points for further investigation. Unfortunately, little of the important work in this field has been published in English, but where adequate English substitutes are available they have been indicated.

Bibliographies

The best way to begin any further study of the subject is to consult the enormous bibliographical information in Friedrich C. Dahlmann and G. Waitz's *Quellenkunde der deutschen Geschichte,* ed. H. Haering and others, 2 v., 9th ed. (Leipzig, 1931–1932). For writings since 1931, see Günther Franz, *Bücherkunde zur deutschen Geschichte* (Munich, 1951). General bibliographical information can also be found in the articles by Polišenský and myself, in the general books by Wedgwood, Pagès, and Friedrich, and in Polišenský's new book, *The Thirty Years' War,* trans. Robert Evans (Berkeley and Los Angeles, 1972). Those among the following works which are marked with an asterisk (*) have useful recent bibliographies on more detailed topics.

Countries

The standard histories of Germany in this period are Moritz Ritter's *Deutsche Geschichte im Zeitalter der Gegenreformation und des dreissigjährigen Krieges, 1555–1648,* 3 v. (Stuttgart, 1889–1908); and Karl Brandi's *Deutsche Geschichte im Zeitalter der Reformation und Gegenreformation,* 3rd ed. (Leipzig, 1942). A good recent English account can be found in Hajo Holborn's *A History of Modern Germany: the Reformation* (New York, 1959). One famous source, referred to by Gustav Freytag and most of those who regard the war as a catastrophe, is now available in an English paperback translation: Johann von Grimmelshausen's *Simplicius Simplicissimus,* tr. George Schulz-Behrend (Indianapolis, 1965; originally published 1669).

For some important areas within Germany the most useful introductions are: on Bavaria, B. Hubensteiner's *Bayerische Geschichte* (Munich, 1950), and Vols. 6 and 7 of Sigmund von Riezler's *Geschichte Bayerns* (Gotha, 1903), as well as the recent studies of Maximilian listed in the section "Protagonists," below; on Brandenburg-Prussia, F. L. Carsten's *The Origins of Prussia* (Oxford, 1954); on the Rhineland, Vol. 4 of Heinrich Boos's *Geschichte der rheinischen Städtekultur von dem Angfang bis zur Gegenwart, mit besonderer Berücksichtigung der Stadt Worms* (Berlin, 1901); and on the Palatinate and its Calvinist policy, the brief introduction by *Claus-Peter Clasen, *The Palatinate in European History, 1559–1660* (Oxford, 1963), F. H. Schubert's important monograph, "Die pfälzische Exilregierung im Driessigjährigen Krieg," *Zeitschrift für Geschichte des Oberrheins* 102 (1954): 575–680, and Schubert's biography of Camerarius, listed below in the section "Protagonists."

On German population during the war the standard work is Günther Franz's *Der Driessigjährige Krieg und das deutsche Volk* (Jena, 1940). The fundamental work on German prices and wages is Moritz J. Elsass, *Umriss einer Geschichte der Preise und Löhne in Deutschland* (Leyden, 1936). For administrative and constitutional history the only important book is *H. F. Schwarz's *The Imperial Privy Council in the Seventeenth Century* (Cambridge, Mass., 1943), which of course deals with the Empire in general, and not just Germany.

For Austrian history in this period, Vol. 1 of H. Hantsch's *Die Geschichte Österreichs,* 2 v., 4th ed. (Graz, 1953–1959) is a conservative but sound survey; *E. Zöllner's *Geschichte Österreichs* (Vienna, 1961) is more imaginative; and Vol. 1 of K. and M. Uhlirz, *Handbuch der Geschichte Österreichs und seiner Nachbarländer Böhmen und Ungarn,* 3 v. (Graz, 1927–1941) is a very thorough account that covers Bohemia and Hungary too.

The best places to start for Bohemian history itself are R. W. Seton-Watson's *A History of the Czechs and Slovaks* (London, 1943); J. V. Polišenský's *History of Czechoslovakia in Outline* (Prague,

1947); *S. H. Thomson's *Czechoslovakia in European History,* 2nd ed. (Princeton, 1953); Vol. 2 of E. Denis' *La Fin de l'Indépendance bohême,* 2 v. (Paris, 1890), and Vol. I. of his *La Bohême depuis la Montagne-Blanche,* 2 v. (Paris, 1903). A recent article that raises some interesting points about the Bohemian émigrés, their hopes and their nationalism, with particular reference to the most famous of the exiles, the influential scholar Jan Comenius, is *B. Šindelář's "Comenius und der Westfälische Friedenskongress," *Historica* 5 (Prague, 1963): 7–107.

Good introductions to French history of the period are Georges Pagès, *Naissance du Grand Siècle* (Paris, 1948); or, in English, *Geoffrey Treasure, *Seventeenth Century France* (New York, 1966). V. L. Tapié's *La politique étrangère de la France et le début de la Guerre de Trente Ans, 1616–1621* (Paris, 1934), B. Baustaedt's *Richelieu und Deutschland . . .* (Berlin, 1936), and L. Batiffol's article, "Richelieu et la question de l'Alsace" in *Revue Historique,* 138 (1921) are important studies on the particular subject of French participation in the war. See, too, the works on Richelieu and Father Joseph mentioned in the section "Protagonists," below.

The best surveys of Spanish history in this period are *John H. Elliott's *Imperial Spain, 1469–1716* (New York, 1964) and vol. II of John Lynch's *Spain Under the Hapsburgs* (Oxford, 1969). The Hapsburg links between Spain and Austria are covered in B. Chudoba's *Spain and the Empire, 1519–1643* (Chicago, 1952). The Spanish-Austrian links during the last years of the war are treated in G. Mecenseffy's monograph, "Habsburger im 17. Jahrhundert. Die Beziehungen der Höfe von Wien und Madrid während des Dreissig-jährigen Krieges," *Archiv für österreichische Geschichte* 121 (1955): 3–91; since she devotes two thirds of the study to the last fourteen years of the war, it provides an excellent complement to Chuboda's book.

On the activities of the Papacy, see L. von Pastor's *The History of of the Popes,* v. 25–31 (London, 1937–1940); *C. C. Eckhardt's *The Papacy and World-Affairs as reflected in the secularization of politics* (Chicago, 1937); D. Albrecht's "Die deutsche Politik Papst Gregors XV," *Schriftenreihe zur Bayerischen Landesgeschichte,* 53 (Munich, 1956); *A. Leman's *Urbain VIII et la rivalité de la France et de la Maison d'Autriche de 1631 à 1635* (Lille, 1920); K. Repgen's "Der päpstliche Protest gegen den Westfälischen Frieden und die Friedenspolitik Urbans VIII.," *Historisches Jahrbuch* 75 (1956): 94–122; and, on the Papacy's financial support of the Emperor and the Catholic cause, D. Albrecht's "Zur Finanzierung des Dreissigjährigen Krieges," *Zeitschrift für bayerischen Landesgeschichte* 19 (1956): 534–567.

The fullest account of English history in this period is S. R. Gardiner's *History of England, from the Accession of James I to the Outbreak of the Civil War, 1603–1642,* 10 v. (London, 1883–1884). A stimulating recent interpretation can be found in *Christopher Hill's *The Century of Revolution, 1603–1714* (London, 1961). On James I, see D. H. Willson, *King James VI and I* (London, 1956)—hardly a protagonist, but important in the early years of the war. On English foreign policy, there is J. V. Polišenský's Czech work *Anglie a Bílá hora* (The Bohemian War and British Policy) (Prague, 1949), J. R. Jones's brief survey, *Britain and Europe in the Seventeenth Century* (New York, 1966), and *C. Albion's *Charles I and the Court of Rome: A Study in 17th century diplomacy* (Louvain, 1935).

Early seventeenth century Dutch history is best approached through P. Geyl's excellent account: *The Netherlands Divided, 1609–1648* (London, 1936; or the second, enlarged edition: *The Netherlands in the Seventeenth Century,* Vol. I: *1601–1648,* New York, 1961). Two excellent short studies of Dutch history in this period are also available, both in paperback: *K. D. H. Haley, *The Dutch in the Seventeenth Century* (New York, 1972), and *Charles Wilson, *The Dutch Republic* (New York, 1968). See, too, the biography of Frederick Henry in the section "Protagonists," below.

The best English account of Swedish history is I. Andersson's *A History of Sweden,* trans. C. Hannay (London, 1955); though of course *Roberts' volumes on Gustavus, from which extracts appear above, give comprehensive coverage through 1632. See, too, Michael Roberts, *Essays in Swedish History* (London, 1967), especially the two essays on Gustavus.

For Danish history in this period, see Vol. V (1559–1648) of Dietrich Schäfer's *Geschichte von Dänemark* (Gotha, 1902): or the briefer, but English, account in J. Danstrup, *A History of Denmark,* tr. V. Lindberg (Copenhagen, 1948). See, too, the biography of Christian IV listed below, in the section "Protagonists."

On Poland, see Oskar Halecki's survey, *A History of Poland,* tr. M. M. Gardner and M. Corbridge-Patkaniowska, 2nd. ed. (New York, 1956); or the more detailed cooperative venture, Vol. I of *The Cambridge History of Poland,* ed. W. F. Reddaway and others (Cambridge, 1950).

A good survey of Russian history in the seventeenth century can be found in S. F. Platonov's *History of Russia,* tr. E. Aronsberg (New York, 1925). On Russia's involvement in the war there it Osip L. Vainstein's Russian work, *Russia and the Thirty Years' War* (Leningrad, 1947).

Finally, on Italy see R. Quazza's *Storia Politica d'Italia, Preponderanza Spagnuola, 1559–1700* (Milan, 1950), as well as his two books on the war in Italy, listed in the next section.

International Relations

A number of works dealing with relations between particular countries have already been mentioned, but the following are studies of international relations in general. The best fairly concise accounts of this period are in Gaston Zeller's *De Christophe Colomb à Cromwell* (v. 2 of *Histoire des Relations Internationales,* ed. Pierre Renouvin, Paris, 1953); W. Platzhoff's *Geschichte des Europäischen Staatensystems, 1559–1660* (Munich, 1928); and, in English, Vol. II of D. J. Hill's *A History of Diplomacy in the International Development of Europe,* 3 v. (London, 1921). Some excellent studies of international negotiations during the war are: *A. van der Essen's *Le Cardinal-Infant et la politique européenne de l'Espagne, 1609–1641,* of which only Vol. I has appeared: *1609–1634* (Louvain, 1944); A. Leman's *Richelieu et Olivares* (Lille, 1938) on Franco-Spanish relations after 1635; two books by Romolo Quazza: *Politica Europea nella Questione Valtellinica: la lega franco-veneto-savoiarda e la pace di Monçon* (Venice, 1921) on the problem of the Valtelline, and *La guerra per la successione di Mantova e del Monferrato, 1628–1631,* 2 v. (Mantua, 1926) on the war of the Mantuan succession; two recent monographs on individual phases of the war: H. Sturmberger's *Aufstand in Böhmen* (Munich and Vienna, 1959), which deals with the period 1618–1621, and D. Albrecht's *Richelieu, Gustav Adolf und das Reich* (Munich and Vienna, 1959), which deals with the Electoral Diet of Regensburg and its consequences; and, finally, *Fritz Dickmann's definitive work on the Peace of Westphalia, and the negotiations leading up to it: *Der Westfälische Frieden* (Münster, 1959). There is also a brief general survey in S. H. Steinberg, *The Thirty Years' War and the Conflict for European Hegemony, 1600–1660* (New York, 1966).

Military History

On general military history see Vol. IV of H. Delbrück's *Geschichte der Kriegskunst im Rahmen der politischen Geschichte* (Berlin, 1920). The best English survey of general military history is O. L. Spaulding, H. Nickerson and J. W. Wright, *Warfare: A Study of Military Methods from the Earliest Times* (New York, 1925). For German military history, see Vol. II of M. Jähns's *Geschichte der Kriegswissenschaften, vornehmlich in Deutschland,* 3 v. (Munich, 1889–1891); and, more recent, two of the volumes in *E. von Frauenholz, Entwicklungsgeschichte des deutschen Heerwesens,* 5 v. (Munich, 1935–1941): Vol. 3, 1: *Das Söldnertum in der Zeit des Dreissigjährigen Krieges,* and Vol. 3,2: *Das Heerwesen in der Zeit des Dreissigjährigen Krieges.* Though mainly a collection of documents, each volume of this last work has an excellent introduction. On Prussian military history, see Vol. I of C. Jany's *Geschichte der königlich preussischen Armee bis zum Jahre 1807,* 5 v. (Berlin, 1928–1937); on the Imperial army, A. Wrede, *Geschichte der kaiserlichen und königlichen Wehrmacht,* 5 v. (Vienna, 1898–1905); on Wallenstein's army, V. Loewe's *Die Organisation und Verwaltung der Wallensteinischen Heere* (Freiburg, 1895); on tactics in the Baltic, R. C. Anderson's *Naval Wars in the Baltic during the sailing-ship epoch, 1522–1850* (London, 1910); and on the general effects of the wars of this period, J. U. Nef's article "War and Economic Progress, 1540–1640," *Economic History Review* 12 (1942).

Protagonists

Many of the above works deal at length with the leading protagonists (e.g. the Popes), but given the organization of this booklet it might be useful to suggest some of the more important specifically biographical studies. The literature on Wallenstein, Gustavus, and Richelieu is fully described in the books from which extracts have been printed; in fact these books are in most cases standard biographies. The exceptions are the monumental biography of Richelieu by G. Hanotaux and the Duc de la Force, *Histoire du Cardinal de Richelieu,* 6 v. (Paris, 1893–1947), and a new, solid, very detailed biography of Wallenstein: *Hellmut Diwald, *Wallenstein: Eine Biographie* (Munich, 1969). As for English biographies, none on Wallenstein or Richelieu are really adequate. Francis Watson's *Wallenstein: Soldier under Saturn* (New York, 1938) is a highly favorable account which ignores some of the most perplexing problems about the General; C. V. Wedgwood's *Richelieu and the French Monarchy* (London, 1949) is excellent reading, but somewhat uncritical; and C. J. Burckhardt's detailed narrative work, *Richelieu and His Age,* 3 v. (New York, 1964–1972) which has been well translated by four different translators. Thanks to *Roberts' volumes, there is no such gap in the literature on Gustavus.

There are few good studies of other leading participants in the war. One of the best served is Maximilian of Bavaria, who is the subject not only of K. Pfister's wide-ranging and colorful biography, *Kurfürst Maximilian von Bayern und sein Jahrhundert* (Munich, 1949), but also of two recent more specialized works: *Helmut Dotterweich's *Der junge Maximilian . . . 1573–1593* (Munich, 1962), and *Dieter Albrecht's important study of Bavarian foreign policy and diplomacy, *Die auswärtige Politik Maximilians von Bayern, 1618–1635* (Göttingen, 1962). Similar work on the other leading statesmen in the Empire, Ferdinand II, Ferdinand III, or John George of Saxony, is sorely lacking. However, an extensive section of Schwarz's book on the Imperial Privy Council, mentioned above, is devoted to biographical sketches of the principal ministers and administrators of the Empire during the seventeenth century. The most convenient place to find some biographical information in English on the Emperor's themselves is Paul Frischauer's *The Imperial Crown,* tr. H. L. Farnell (London, 1939); or see the brief survey in *A. Wandruszka, *The House of Habsburg: Six Hundred Years of a European Dynasty,* tr. C. and H. Epstein (New York, 1964). Two more specialized works also deserve mention: Gertrude von Schwarzenfeld's biography of Rudolf II, *Rudolf II, Der Saturnische Kaiser* (Munich, 1961); and an excellent little study of Ferdinand II's constitutional ideas: H. Sturmberger's *Kaiser Ferdinand II und das Problem des Absolutismus* (Vienna, 1957). The only good biography of a Protestant leader in the Empire is *F. H. Schubert's *Ludwig Camerarius (1573–1651). Eine Biographie* (Kallmünz, 1955).

The generals such as Tilly, Mansfeld and Arnim have been neglected by recent scholarship, but there is an exhaustive study of Christian of Halberstadt's campaigns: A. Wertheim's *Der tolle Halberstädter Herzog, Christian von Braunschweig,* 2 v. (Berlin, 1929).

In conclusion, the following books on important non-Germans who were deeply involved in the war should be noted: *G. Marañón's *El conde-duque de Olivares,* 3rd ed. (Madrid, 1952) on Spain's chief minister; G. Fagniez, *Le Père Joseph et Richelieu,* 2 v. (Paris, 1894) on Richelieu's indefatigable assistant; P. J. Blok, *Frederik Hendrik, Prins Van Oranje* (Amsterdam, 1924) on the Dutch leader; and John A. Gade's colorful *Christian IV, King of Denmark and Norway: a Picture of the Seventeenth Century* (Boston and New York, 1928).

N.B. There has now appeared, just in time for inclusion here, a good short biography of Richelieu in English: *G. R. R. Treasure, *Cardinal Richelieu* (London, 1972).